# The Book of Korean Shijo

---

Harvard East Asian Monographs 215

Harvard-Ewha Series on Korea

## Harvard-Ewha Series on Korea

The Harvard-Ewha Series on Korea, published by the Harvard University Asia Center, is supported by the Korea Institute of Harvard University, Cambridge, Massachusetts, and by Ewha Woman's University, Seoul, Korea. It is committed to the publication of outstanding new work in both the humanities and the social sciences, including new scholarship in such areas as literature, intellectual and cultural history, and gender studies.

Professor Carter Eckert
Director
Korea Institute, Harvard University

Reverend Professor Sang Chang
President
Ewha Woman's University

# The Book of Korean Shijo

Translated and edited by

## Kevin O'Rourke

Published by the Harvard University Asia Center
and distributed by Harvard University Press
Cambridge (Massachusetts) and London 2002

Printed in the United States of America

The Harvard University Asia Center publishes a monograph series and, in coordination with the Fairbank Center for East Asian Research, the Korea Institute, the Reischauer Institute of Japanese Studies, and other faculties and institutes, administers research projects designed to further scholarly understanding of China, Japan, Vietnam, Korea, and other Asian countries. The Center also sponsors projects addressing multidisciplinary and regional issues in Asia.

Library of Congress Cataloging-in-Publication Data
The book of Korean Shijo / translated and edited by Kevin O'Rourke.
    p. cm. -- (Harvard East Asian monographs ; 215)
    Includes bibliographic references and index.
    ISBN 0-674-00857-x (cl : alk. paper)
      1. Sijo--Translations into English. 2. Korean poetry--To 1900--Translations into English. 3. Sijo--History and criticism. 4. Poets, Korean. I. O'Rourke, Kevin. II. Series.

PL984.E3 B66 2002
895.7'1008--dc21                                           2002017339

Indexes by the author

☯    Printed on acid-free paper

Last figure below indicates year of this printing
12  11  10  09  08  07  06  05  04  03  02

*For Frank and Rose*

Hardly a day goes by that I don't recall
the Song poet's lament for seventy years
of listening without understanding to the patter of spring rain in the river.
I listen on
hoping for the flash of that elusive harmonics of the heart.

# Acknowledgments

Sincere thanks are due to a host of colleagues and friends. I am particularly indebted to Professor Kim Chinyong of Kyunghee University for his help in interpreting difficult texts and to the students of the English Department of Kyunghee University for their help in editing the manuscript. I am also indebted to Professor Park Kidawk for much help in elucidating texts and to Han Kyongshim for unstinting efforts to track down sources and elusive references.

Acknowledgment is made of the support of the Korean Culture and Arts Foundation in the making of the translations. Poems in this collection have previously appeared in the *Korea Herald, Korea Times, Korea Journal, Koreana, Hemisphere, Southern Review,* and *Translation.*

K.O'R.

# Contents

Introduction    1

Texts and Sources    23

*Part I    Songs from Koryŏ (918–1392)   27*

Ch'oe Ch'ung    27

Yi Kyubo    28

U T'ak    28

Yi Cho'nyŏn    29

Ch'oe Yŏng    29

Yi Saek    30

Yi Chik    30

Yi Pang'wŏn    31

Chŏng Mongju    31

Chŏng Mongju's mother    32

Yi Chono    32

Chŏng Tojŏn    33

*Part II    Chosŏn Dynasty: Foundation to the
Hideyoshi War (1392–1592)   37*

Cho Chun    37

Kil Chae    38

Maeng Sasŏng    38

Hwang Hŭi    39

Ha Wiji                                                    40

Wŏn Ch'ŏnsŏk                                               40

Kim Chongsŏ                                                41

Yi Kae                                                     41

Pak P'aengnyŏn                                             42

Sŏng Sammun                                                43

Yu Ŭngbu                                                   43

Yu Sŏng'wŏn                                                44

Tanjong                                                    44

Kim Koengp'il                                              45

Wang Pang'yŏn                                              45

Wŏn Ho                                                     46

Prince Wŏlsan                                              46

Yi Hyŏnbo                                                  46

Chŏng Hŭiryang                                             48

Kim Ku                                                     48

Sŏ Kyŏngdŏk                                                49

Song Sun                                                   50

An Chŏng                                                   51

Sŏng Un                                                    51

Yi Hwang                                                   51

Cho Shik                                                   54

Hwang Chini                                                55

Kim Inhu                                                   56

Yu Hŭich'un                                                57

Song In                                                    57

Yang Saŏn                                                  58

Yang Ŭngjŏng                                               58

Yi Hubaek                                                  59

Kang Ik                                                    59

Kim Sŏng'wŏn 60

Kwŏn Homun 60

Yi Yangwŏn 62

Yu Chashin 62

Sŏng Hon 63

Yi I 63

Chŏng Ch'ŏl 65

Sŏ Ik 75

Han Ho 76

Cho Hŏn 76

Yi Sunshin 77

Kim Changsaeng 77

Im Che 77

Hanu 78

Sŏnjo 78

Cho Chonsŏng 79

Song T'a 79

Yi Tŏkhyŏng 80

Yi Tŏg'il 80

Kim Sang'yŏng 80

Pak Inno 81

Kang Pokchung 83

Shin Hŭm 84

Chang Man 86

Kim Tŏngnyŏng 87

Chŏng On 87

Kim Kwang'uk 88

Kim Yuk 89

Hong Ikhan 90

Yun Sŏndo 90

Part III    Choson Dynasty: After the Hideyoshi
            War (1592–1910)   111

Yi Myŏnghan                                          111
Chŏng Tugyŏng                                        112
Hong Nang                                            112
Chŏng T'aehwa                                        112
Yi Yŏng                                              113
Hyojong                                              113
Prince Inp'yŏng                                      113
Nam Kuman                                            114
Prince Nang'wŏn                                      114
Prince Yuch'ŏn                                       115
Pak T'aebo                                           115
Kim Ch'ang'ŏp                                        115
Chu Ŭishik                                           116
An Sŏu                                               116
Yun Tusŏ                                             117
Kim Ch'ŏnt'aek                                       117
Yun Sun                                              119
Kim Sujang                                           120
Kim Ugyu                                             132
Yi Chŏngbo                                           132
Cho Myŏngni                                          137
Yi Chae                                              137
Hwang Yunsŏk                                         137
Shin Hŏnjo                                           138
Shin Wi                                              138
Pak Hyogwan                                          139
Kim Samhyŏn                                          140
Songgyeyŏnwŏl                                        141
Kim Chint'ae                                         142

Kim Sŏnggi                                                143

Kim Yŏng                                                 144

Yi Chŏngjin                                              144

Kim Yugi                                                 145

Kim Sŏngch'oe                                           145

An Minyŏng                                              145

Yi Sebo                                                  148

Yi Chaemyŏn                                             150

Cho Hwang                                               150

Ch'oe Chikt'ae                                          151

Na Chisŏng                                              151

Yi Chungjip                                             151

An Yŏnbo                                                152

Ho Sŏkkyun                                              152

Yi P'ansŏ In'ŭng                                        152

Kim Ch'iu                                               153

Kim Hag'yŏn                                             153

Ha Sunil                                                153

Kwŏn Ingnyung                                          154

Ch'ŏn'gŭm                                               154

Maehwa                                                  154

Hongjang                                                155

Chin'ok                                                 155

Part IV    *Anonymous Songs*   *159*

Moral Songs                                             160

Drinking Songs                                          167

Songs of Nature                                         170

Songs of Mortality                                      175

Love Songs                                              178

Songs of Parting                                        193

## Reference Matter

*Chronology of the Chosŏn Dynasty Kings*                    201

*Bibliography*                                             203

*Index of Poets*                                          205

*Index of First Lines*                                    207

# The Book of Korean Shijo

# Introduction

Cho Kyuik begins his study of the *kagok-ch'angsa* (literally *kagok*-song-lyric, his preferred term for the genre more commonly called *shijo*) by pointing out that Korea has two poetry traditions: the *hanshi* tradition (poems in Chinese following the rules of Chinese prosody), a poetry to be read and contemplated; and the vernacular tradition (*hyangga*, Koryŏ *kayo*, *kasa*, and what today we call *shijo*), a poetry to be sung and heard. The common denominator across the vernacular songs, he tells us, is the *kasa*, literally "music-words." All vernacular songs were *kasa*. The songs we call *shijo* today are a subdivision of *kasa*, and they were originally sung to the *kagok-ch'ang*. The *shijo-ch'ang*, it is surmised, did not develop until the middle of the nineteenth century.[1]

According to Yi Pyŏnggi, the first use of the term *shijo* occurs in a record written by Shin Kwangsu (1712–75), who mentions that *shijo* began with Yi Sech'un, a well-known contemporary singer.[2] This reference is not to a literary genre but to the title of a tune.[3] The term seems to have been a shortened version of *shijŏlgajo*, meaning "popular seasonal songs."[4] An Chasan did not use the term *shijo* in his *Chosŏn munhaksa* (History of Chosŏn literature; 1922), which was the first modern scholarly treatment of the history of Korean literature; instead, he called these songs *kasa* throughout this work. However, in later papers and in *Shijo shihak* (The poetics of *shijo*; 1949), the

1. Cho Kyuik, *Kagokch'angsaŭi kungmunhakchŏk ponjil* (The essence of the *kagok-ch'ang* song lyric in the Korean literature tradition) (Seoul: Chimmundang, 1994), pp. 19–77.

2. Yi Pyŏnggi, *Shijoŭi palsaenggwa kagokkwaŭi kubun* (The development of *shijo* and the distinction from *kagok*) (Seoul: Chindanhakbu, 1934), 1: 113–44.

3. Chŏng Pyŏng'uk, *Han'guk kojŏn shigaron* (A study of classical Korean poetry) (Seoul: Shin'gu munhwasa, 1988), p. 177.

4. Yi Pyŏnggi, pp. 113–44.

first full-length book on *shijo*, he used the term *shijo* extensively. Thus it would seem that the term *shijo*, as a generic reference to a literary text, began to be used in the 1920s, presumably with the beginning of the *shijo* revival movement, which dates from Ch'oe Namsŏn's 1926 article "Chosŏn kungmin munhakŭroŭi shijo" (*Shijo* as the national literature of Chosŏn).[5] The term *shijo* came into vogue at this time in order to distinguish traditional verse from the flood of Western poetry that had begun to sweep the Korean literary stage.[6] Previously, terms such as *tan'ga, shinbon, changdan'ga, shinjo,* and *shiyo* had been used to denote traditional verse. As a term of reference to a musical tradition, however, *shijo* was presumably already in wide use. By the end of the 1920s, the *shijo-ch'ang* had replaced the *kagok-ch'ang* as the popular performance mode for *shijo*.[7] One Korean gentleman has told me that in the late 1920s or early 1930s his mother used the term *shijo* disparagingly of the menfolk of the house. "They've gone *shijo-ing*," she would say, the inference being they were wasting their time on silly songs. It is a significant comment because it indicates that in the popular awareness *shijo* was a song form rather than a literary text.

The 1920s were a period of prodigious literary activity in Korea. Young intellectuals, trained in Japanese universities, were beginning to introduce the new literature from the West. In the initial phase, the interests of those propagating the new literature were more national than literary. They showed no interest in *shijo* until about 1925.[8] Ch'oe Namsŏn and Yi Kwang-su, who were among the most prominent of the rising generation, were the first to see the inherent possibilities of the uniquely Korean *shijo* as a vehicle for raising national consciousness against the backdrop of Japanese oppression. This was the genesis of the *shijo* revival, a movement that was, in effect, a nationalist response to the nation's colonial status. The movement expressed itself in a drive to preserve a unique Korean identity. The essays by the leaders of the *shijo* revival in Lee T'aeguk's *Shijo yŏn'gu nonch'ŏng* (Compendium of *shijo* studies; 1950) attest to the pivotal place these early scholars assigned to *shijo* as a cultural vehicle for passing on the native Korean tradi-

---

5. Ch'oe Namsŏn, "Chosŏn kungmin munhakŭroŭi shijo" (*Shijo* as the national literature of Chosŏn), *Chosŏn mundan*, no. 16 (May 1926).

6. Chŏng Pyŏng'uk, p. 177.

7. Cho Kyuik, p. 58.

8. Paek Ch'ŏl, *Paek Ch'ŏl munhak chŏnjip* (Paek Ch'ŏl literary miscellany) (Seoul: Shin'gu munhwasa, 1968), p. 363.

tion. *Shijo* could have been promoted as a musical movement, but the advance of printing technology saw to it that *shijo* was defined as a written text.[9]

Spurred by enthusiasm for the *shijo* revival movement, Yi Kwangsu, Ch'oe Namsŏn, An Chasan, Yi Pyŏnggi, Yi Ŭnsang, and Cho Yunche quickly developed a criticism of *shijo* as literary text, a criticism that remained virtually unchallenged for the next generation. The *shijo* was more than a song, it was claimed, it was a literary text, the most traditional of Korean literary forms. The novelist Yŏm Sangsŏp declared that *shijo* contains "the breath of the Chosŏn people, the soul of the Chosŏn people," a sentiment echoed loudly throughout the nationalist camp.[10] Ch'oe Namsŏn's "Shijoryu" (*Shijo*) recorded the poems for the first time in a three-*chang* format. Yi Pyŏnggi popularized the terms "opening *chang*," "middle *chang*," and "final *chang*."[11] The three-*chang* division became standard in *shijo* criticism, with much debate among scholars on the critical terminology of *chang* (unit), *ku* (division of unit), and *ŭmbo* (breath group). Yi Kwangsu and An Chasan suggested a three-*chang*, six-*ku* pattern; Yi Pyŏnggi proposed a three-*chang*, eight-*ku* pattern; Yi Ŭnsang advocated a three-*chang*, twelve-*ku* pattern. Cho Yunche's article "Shijo chasu ko" (Study of syllable count in *shijo*; *Shinhŭng*, 1931.4) proved to be the definitive treatment of *shijo* rhythmical structure in this early period. He also suggested a three-*chang*, twelve-*ku* pattern, but his pattern was more elastic and at the same time more comprehensive than those advanced by his colleagues. In addition to giving the ideal count, he also specified the minimum and maximum values; in the following list Cho's ideal count is shown first, followed by the minimum and maximum values in parentheses.[12]

| *chang* | 1 *ku* | 2 *ku* | 3 *ku* | 4 *ku* |
|---|---|---|---|---|
| 1st | 3 (2–4) | 4 (4–6) | 4,3 (2–5) | 4 (4–6) |
| 2nd | 3 (1–4) | 4 (3–6) | 4,3 (2–5) | 4 (4–6) |
| 3rd | 3 (3) | 5 (5–9) | 4 (4–5) | 3 (3–4) |

9. Kim Taehaeng, *Shijo yuhyŏngnon* (Studies of form in *shijo*) (Seoul: Ewha University Press, 1986), p. 35.

10. Yŏm Sangsŏp, *Chosŏn ilbo*, Dec. 1926.

11. Yi Pyŏnggi, "Shijoran muŏshin'ga" (What is *shijo*), *Tonga ilbo*, Dec. 10–11, 1926; and idem, "Shijo wŏllyuron" (A study of the original form of *shijo*), *Shinsaeng*, no. 4 (1929).

12. Cho Yunche, *Chosŏn shigaŭi yŏn'gu* (A study of Chosŏn poetry) (Seoul: Chisŏmunhwasa, 1948), p. 172.

The essential criteria of the literary *shijo* were now firmly established. *Shijo* was a three-*chang* poem, with fourteen to sixteen syllables in each *chang*, distributed through four distinct *ŭmbo*, or breath groups, with no more than forty-five syllables. The first *ku* of the final *chang* invariably had three syllables; the second *ku* of the final *chang* not less than five syllables. This was the regular or ordinary *shijo*, called *p'yŏng shijo*. Two variations of the basic form were postulated: the *ŏt shijo*, in which the first or the second *chang* might be somewhat extended; and the *sasŏl shijo*, in which all three *chang* might be extended. These opinions held sway for a generation. By the 1950s, however, scholars began questioning the enormous number of exceptions to the ideal count as postulated in the various syllable-count systems. Consequently, several new theories of the rhythmic structure of *shijo* were introduced. The new theories ran the gamut of prosodic possibility: an English-style metric line with accented and unaccented syllables; and two explanations reflecting the Chinese tradition of prosody, one based on pitch (tone) and the other on duration or quantity (*changdan*: long, short).[13] None of these theories provided real satisfaction. Writing in the 1970s, Kim Chehyŏn summarized the confusion that persisted in *shijo* studies: "As yet, not only has the concept and function of *chang*, *ku*, and *ŭmbo* not been clarified, but the three-*chang* structural principle has not been adequately elucidated."[14] Ultimately, all that could be said with certainty about the rhythm of *shijo* was that the *ŭmbo* is the fundamental unit and that all Korean writing, both prose and poetry, utilizes a 3,4 rhythm.[15]

Since the 1920s critics have vigorously debated the origin of the form. *Shijo* is seen variously as a development of Shilla *hyangga*, of the Koryŏ *tan'ga*, or of the shamanistic chants of antiquity; a form that developed naturally in the course of translating Chinese poems into Korean; or a form that derives from Buddhist songs from China. These have been the traditional approaches. In recent years, however, as more and more attention has being paid to the musical aspects of *shijo*, scholars have begun to look for the sources of *shijo* in the musical tradition.[16]

---

13. For a full discussion of these various theories, see Chŏng Pyŏng'uk, *Han'guk shigaŭi unyulgwa hyŏngt'ae* (Rhythm and form in Korean poetry) (Seoul: Semunsa, 1984), pp. 9–33; and Kim Chinu, "Shijoŭi unyul kujoŭi saegoch'al" (A new study of the structure of *shijo* rhythm), 'Han'gŭl' 60 tol ki'nyŏm t'ŭkchip 1 (1981): 173–74.

14. Kim Chehyŏn, *Shijo munhangnon* (A study of *shijo* literature) (Seoul: Yejŏnsa, 1975), p. 42.

15. Ibid., pp. 28–33.

16. Kim Taehaeng, pp. 50–97.

*Shijo* is so totally Korean in its sensibility that commentators have always been reluctant to see its source in a foreign tradition. Hence, they have consistently refused to accept the theory that *shijo* emerged in the process of translating Chinese quatrains. Correspondences with *shijo* are noted in the four-part structure of the quatrain (*ki, sŭng, chŏn, kyŏl*: introduction, development, twist, and conclusion) and in the fact that, much like the *shijo ku*, *hanshi* employed a seven-syllable or five-syllable line. However, as critics are quick to point out, this is the structure of all Korean lyric poetry, and the correspondence with the *shijo ku* is superficial.

A native origin for *shijo* has had more adherents. Many scholars have proposed *hyangga* as the source. They base their view on the three-part, ten-*ku* structure of the *hyangga*, which resembles the three-*chang* structure of the *shijo*. They also point to the first *ŭmbo* in the final *chang*: in both *hyangga* and *shijo*, this has three syllables and is often an exclamation.[17] Korea's ancient shamanistic songs are also proposed as the origin of *shijo*: proponents of this view cite the similar three-*chang*, four-*ŭmbo* structure and also the similar three-syllable first *ku* in the final *chang*.[18]

The theory that *shijo* developed from Koryŏ *tan'ga* has also enjoyed consistent support from scholars through the years.[19] Literary forms do not grow in a vacuum, proponents of this view say. Since *shijo* is a song genre that reached its full development in the Chosŏn dynasty, it would seem most likely that it developed from the popular songs of the preceding Koryŏ dynasty. The songs would have been composed by the newly emerged class of *sadaebu* (scholar-officials), who came to power with the military takeover at the end of the twelfth century in Koryŏ. In support of their claims, they cite the songs in the great anthologies that purport to date from Koryŏ times. Opponents of this view insist there is no critical evidence to support such claims: the ascriptions in the great anthologies cannot be accepted at face value, nor is there any evidence to show how *shijo* developed from Koryŏ popular songs. The argument for a *tan'ga* origin rests totally on historical documents, and if earlier documentation is discovered, the argument disintegrates.

The failure of scholars to demonstrate beyond a reasonable doubt the theories of an origin in traditional forms emboldened theorists in the

---

17. Kim Chehyŏn, p. 142.
18. Ibid., p. 143.
19. Kim Taehaeng, pp. 48–49.

last quarter of the twentieth century to suggest that *shijo* may not have developed until the fifteenth and sixteenth centuries. They base their opinions on the lack of documentation dating from Koryŏ and earlier in contrast to the abundance of historical records in Chosŏn. Accordingly, it is now suggested that something more than mere historical documentation is demanded. Scholars should also look for the source of *shijo* in the musical tradition of Koryŏ.

There are two main lines of argument: one traces the musical tradition to *Taeyŏp* (*Mandaeyŏp, Chungdaeyŏp,* and *Saktaeyŏp*), songs popular in Koryŏ; the other suggests tentatively that *Pukchŏn,* a tune performed in the royal palace during the reign of Ch'unghye at the end of Koryŏ, is the ancestor of *shijo.* Most of the songbooks that introduce *shijo* texts and melodies mention *Taeyŏp* and *Pukchŏn* as among the earliest melodies. Most of them say further that *Mandaeyŏp* and *Chungdaeyŏp* are earlier than *Pukchŏn.* It is also clear that *Taeyŏp* is associated with the *kagok-ch'ang,* and *Pukchŏn* with the *shijo-ch'ang.* Yi Ik (1681–1763) says that *Taeyŏp* was originally called *Shimbanggok.* It is not totally clear whether *Shimbanggok* refers to the melody of *Chungdaeyŏp* or to text and melody. Later songbooks, however, almost invariably feature melody and text together under the title *Shimbanggok.* Thus scholars today are inclined to believe that *Shimbanggok* is the original *shijo* music and the ancestor of the *shijo* text. The musical question is vastly complicated.[20]

The difficulty of unraveling the history of *shijo* is compounded by the fact that *han'gŭl* was not invented until 1446. If one holds the view that *shijo* date to Koryŏ or earlier, one must accept that poems written prior to 1446 either were recorded originally in Chinese and only subsequently translated or retranslated into Korean or were recorded orally from the beginning. The problem is further complicated by the facts that the first of the great anthologies, *Ch'ŏnggu yŏng'ŏn,* was not published until 1728 and that *shijo* by individual poets appeared in posthumous collections, many of them produced long after the death of the poet.

What can we say with certainty about the *shijo* form prior to its emergence as a literary text in the twentieth century? The following are the central facts.

---

20. For a summary of the issues, see Kwŏn Tuhwan, "Shijoŭi palsaenggwa kiwŏn" (Emergence and origin of *shijo*), in Kungmunhakhoe, ed., *Koshijo yŏn'gu* (Classical *shijo* studies) (Seoul: T'aehaksa, 1997), pp. 9–32.

1. No classical document refers to the three-*chang*, fixed-form poem of approximately forty-five syllables we know today as *shijo*.[21]

2. Less than twenty songs that purport to date to Koryŏ are recorded, and they are recorded in the great *shijo* anthologies, which date from the eighteenth century. Ch'oe Tongwŏn says only eight Koryŏ poets have credible credentials: U T'ak, Yi Cho'nyŏn, Ch'oe Yŏng, Sŏng Yŏwan, Chŏng Mongju, Yi Chono, Yi Saek, and T'aejong.[22] Kwŏn Tuhwan doubts the ascription of the song Yi Pang'wŏn wrote to lure Chŏng Mongju from his loyalty to Koryŏ; he also doubts the ascription of Chŏng Mongju's defiant answering song.[23]

3. Many short songs from early Chosŏn survive; they are recorded in private *munjip* (collections) and in the great anthologies. However, they are not called *shijo*.

4. Han'gŭl was invented in the reign of Sejong (fifteenth century); before this time all songs were recorded in Chinese or transmitted orally. This accounts for some of the difficulties of ascription.

5. In the anthologies and the private *munjip*, the songs are recorded variously in Chinese, *han'gŭl*, or a mixture of Chinese and *han'gŭl*. Again they are not called *shijo*.

6. The songs can be sung to a *kagok-ch'ang* or a *shijo-ch'ang*. The *kagok-ch'ang* has five sung *chang* and two instrumental interludes (*chungyŏŭm* and *taeyŏŭm*): the music is complex, difficult to perform, and demands a large number of players. Only a professional can sing this music. An added difficulty arises from the wide range of *kagok* tunes that the *kagok-ch'ang* employed. The *shijo-ch'ang*, on the other hand is much easier to perform. It has only four song melodies.[24] The music is so simple that a singer can tap the time out on his thigh and produce the *shijo hŭng* (excitement) feeling with relative ease.[25] The length of the *chang* text was pivotal in performance of the *shijo-ch'ang*: neither a very short *chang* nor a very long first or third *chang* could be sung to the *shijo-ch'ang*, whereas the middle *chang*, no matter how long, could always be performed.[26] The *kagok-ch'ang* did not have these problems.

---

21. Cho Kyuik, p. 424.

22. Ch'oe Tongwŏn, *Koshijo non'go* (Studies in classical *shijo*) (Seoul: Samyŏngsa, 1990), p. 17.

23. Kwŏn Tuhwan, p. 10.

24. Ch'oe Tongwŏn, p. 248.

25. Chŏn Kyut'ae, *Han'guk shiga yŏn'gu* (Studies in Korean poetry) (Seoul: Koryŏwŏn, 1986), p. 479.

26. Kim Sangsŏn, *Han'guk shiga hyŏngt'aeron* (A study of form in Korean poetry) (Seoul: Ilchogak, 1979), pp. 152–53.

7. *Ch'ŏnggu yŏng'ŏn* compiled by Kim Ch'ŏnt'aek (1728), *Haedong kayo* compiled by Kim Sujang (1763), and *Kagok wŏllyu* compiled by Pak Hyogwan and An Minyŏng (1876) are the three great anthologies. Both *Ch'ŏnggu yŏng'ŏn* and *Haedong kayo* record the poems in continuous prose formats. *Kagok wŏllyu*, however, presents the poems in a five-*chang* format. All three anthologies order the poems around the music. The recording of the songs in prose form in *Ch'ŏnggu yŏng'ŏn* indicates that Kim Ch'ŏnt'aek's main interest was in compiling a songbook. He gave six songs. The individual *shijo* may be sung to any of these songs.[27] It seems fair to conclude that Kim Sujang's main interest was also in the creation of a songbook rather than a literary text. It is noteworthy that all three major anthologies are *kagok-ch'ang* songbooks. However, there are also songbooks that are thought to be *shijo-ch'ang* songbooks, notably *P'unga*, compiled by Yi Sebo in 1862, *Shijo kwansŏbon*, *Shijo kasa*, *Shiyo*, and *Namhunt'aep'yŏngga*. With the exception of *P'unga*, no dates are available for these songbooks, but they are believed to be *shijo-ch'ang* songbooks because they cut the last *ku* of the final *chang*. *Samjukkŭmbo* is a *shijo-ch'ang* songbook that records the texts in a five-*chang* pattern.[28]

8. *Kagok wŏllyu* arranged its texts in the five-*chang* division of the *kagok-ch'ang*. It seems certain that the majority of *shijo* currently extant were sung originally to the *kagok-ch'ang*.[29] Because of difficulty of performance, the five-*chang* kagok-ch'ang* went into decline around the time of Pak Hyogwan and An Minyŏng, that is, toward the end of the nineteenth century, when the composition of *shijo* was already in decline. In the meantime a simple three-*chang* shijo-ch'ang* had been developed. We cannot be certain when the three-*chang* shijo-ch'ang* first appeared, but it was in use during the mid-nineteenth century. An Minyŏng attests to this in a book of his songs, *Kŭmokch'ongbu*, in which he recorded his impressions of a performance of the three-*chang* shijo-ch'ang*. Professionals like Pak Hyogwan and An Minyŏng continued to perform the older *kagok-ch'ang*—presumably they had no choice, because it was their livelihood—but the *shijo-ch'ang* eventually replaced the *kagok-ch'ang* as the premier performance mode for *shijo*. The process was gradual, continu-

---

27. Chŏng Chaeho; Kungmunhakhoe, ed., *Ch'ŏnggu yŏng'ŏn p'yŏnch'an ŭishik ko* (*Ch'ŏnggu yŏng'ŏn*: a study of editorial awareness), p. 294.

28. Cho Kyuik, p. 57.

29. Ibid., p. 46.

ing over a period of sixty or seventy years, but by the end of the 1920s, the *shijo-ch'ang* had completely replaced the *kagok-ch'ang*.[30]

9. The new *shijo-ch'ang* appears to be the basis for the modern three-*chang* division of *shijo* adopted by Ch'oe Namsŏn and subsequent commentators.[31]

Twentieth-century scholars treated the *shijo* almost exclusively as literary text and paid only lip service to the music. This has changed in recent years, and considerable efforts have been made to elucidate the musical background of the form. All are agreed that the music was originally integral to the form. Vernacular Korean poetry was meant to be sung and heard rather than to be read and contemplated. The vernacular songs were supposed to move the heart, rather than the head, to generate a mood of *hŭng*, that sense of tingling excitement mentioned by so many Korean poets.[32] The inference is obvious: *shijo* was more for entertainment than for literary purposes. The fact that they were composed in *ŏnmun* (vulgar speech) and that Chinese remained the language of literature until the end of the nineteenth century adds more weight to the *shijo* as entertainment argument.

Although the *shijo* originated as song, *shijo* is today treated primarily as a literary text, a short lyric poem, read and contemplated rather than performed and heard. Furthermore, the three-*chang* division of the *shijo* text introduced by Ch'oe Namsŏn is so imbedded in the popular consciousness as to be virtually unassailable. Accordingly, the translations in this volume employ the three-*chang* structure, in combination with a five-line English format that corresponds broadly with the five-part structure of the *kagok-ch'ang* to which the songs were originally sung. Lines 1 and 2 in the translations are the opening *chang*; line 3 is the middle *chang*; and lines 4 and 5 are the final *chang*. The five-line format is primarily a visual device. No claim is being made that the musical structure and the poetical structure are one. Nor is there any possibility of performing these English songs to the *kagok-ch'ang*. This would be patently ridiculous. I developed the five-line English format not only because it was warranted by the history of the *shijo*, but also because it opens up huge possibilities in English; it is new and exciting, as the *shijo* should be for the English reader, a much superior vehicle to the traditional English translation vehicle, the pretty six-line lyric. The translations attempt

---

30. For a full account of *kagok-ch'ang* and *shijo-ch'ang*, see Cho Kyuik, pp. 56–72.
31. Ibid., p. 58.
32. Ibid., p. 34.

to get something of the feel of the *kagok* back into the literary text, to approximate in English the Korean sense of *hŭng* that is at the heart of the *shijo* experience.

The five-line format in English translation gives *shijo* a special feel on the written page, an individuality that takes *shijo* outside the norm of English poetry. This is of the utmost importance. There is nothing in English poetry remotely like the *shijo*, but unfortunately traditional *shijo* translations do not make this clear: they tend to present the *shijo* as an elongated haiku, couched in a nice six-line English lyric. The five-line format, however, allows the translator to bring the uniqueness of the *shijo* home to the reader through the appearance of the *shijo* on the page. The shape of the *shijo* and the *shijo's* prosy-recitative quality comes across in a way not hitherto possible: the unusual five-line format, the varying line lengths, especially the longer third and fifth lines, and the three-syllable fourth line all contribute to presenting something uniquely Korean, and at the same time something totally new in English.

The five-line format, however, does have its problems. The most obvious is the fourth line, which is normally not semantically independent. I have had to reach an accommodation between musical development and the truncated three-syllable literary text. It is difficult to formulate a consistent English practice that reflects the strict three-syllable count of the Korean without descending into nonsense. Accordingly, in the English versions the fourth line exhibits some variety in syllable count. Common sense supersedes mathematical considerations. The translations favor a format that makes visual sense on the page: they retain the truncated feel of the first *ku* of the final *chang* by using a short fourth line and try to convey the special quality of the longer middle and final *chang* by using longer third and fifth lines. However, when the third line in the English version seems out of balance visually with the rest of the poem, for example, when an excessively long third line is combined with a short fifth line, I have broken the third line, using indentation to indicate the run-on. Occasionally, the first, second or fifth line is also broken; again indentation marks the run-on. The general principle has been to preserve the shape and feel of the original, while taking care to create a poem that looks well on the page. If this has meant taking liberties in some cases with the pattern of *shijo* I have established, I have not hesitated to do so.

*Shijo* are songs. This gives them a particular quality: they are light, personal, and often conversational; the language is simple, direct, and devoid of elaboration or ornamentation. The *shijo* poet gives a firsthand account of his own personal experience of life and emotion: the rise and fall of dynasties; loyalty to the king; friendship, love, and parting; the pleasures of wine; the beauty and transience of human existence; the inexorable advance of old age.

The opening *chang* of a *shijo* poem presents an idea or an image, usually in the form of a general statement:

> In this world medicine is plentiful
> and sharp knives abound, they say.

Or, a second example:

> Ride a horse through a field of flowers
> and the scent lingers on the hoof.

Normally, no context is given for this general statement, although this does not hold true as a general norm. When some context is provided or hinted at, the amount of detail given obviously varies from poem to poem:

> My horse is neighing for the road,
> but my love won't let me go.

Clearly, two people are involved, the man who feels it is time to go and his ladylove who wants him to tarry. Sometimes, context is hinted through implication rather than through direct statement:

> Look at that girl in blouse and patterned skirt,
> her face prettily powdered, her hair as yet unpinned.

The reader immediately realizes that the girl is pretty and that her face is painted; a Korean reader would know that she is unmarried because her hair is unpinned. However, the reader may not be aware of the implications of "patterned skirt." Korean ladies might wear patterned blouses but not patterned skirts. To wear a patterned skirt was unseemly, something a girl from a good family would not do. Thus, the opening *chang* of this poem points at the girl's moral attitude and notes that it leaves something to be desired.

The middle *chang* develops the content of the opening *chang*. This development can occur in a number of ways. First, it can occur by providing a context where none has been given:

> In this world medicine is plentiful
> and sharp knives abound, they say,
> but there's no knife to cut off affection, no medicine to forget true love.

Second, development can be achieved by introducing new material:

> Ride a horse through a field of flowers
> and the scent lingers on the hoof.
> Enter a wine-spring tavern and the smell of undrunk wine sticks fast.

The two images are always related, that is, they are similar in kind. In poems structured after this pattern, context is usually hinted at first, and a full statement is reserved till later.

Third, development can occur by providing more detail on a particular context:

> My horse is neighing for the road,
> but my love won't let me go.
> The sun is crossing the mountain and I've a thousand *li* to go.

Additional information is given on the time of day and the length of the journey facing the speaker. In poem four, the suspicions aroused by the use of the word "patterned" are proved correct in the middle *chang*.

> Look at that girl in blouse and patterned skirt,
> her face prettily powdered, her hair as yet unpinned.
> Yesterday she deceived me and now she's off to deceive another,

This poem is exceptional in terms of full statement of context given at this stage of the development of the imagery.

The first *ku* of the final *chang* (line 4) is referred to as the "twist." Often it is no more than a conventional phrase such as *So be it*, but it serves as counterpoint to the irony that is so often characteristic of the second part of the final *chang* (line 5 in the translations in this book). Irony acts as catalyst in the fusion of image and idea in order to present some concrete aspect of the poet's experience. The conclusion is an amalgam of wit and sensibility.

Some commentators have pointed out that *shijo* in translation sometimes appear inconclusive. This is quite true. There are two reasons this happens: either the translation is poor and the translator has not understood all the ironic levels of meaning, or the original poem is not a good example of the genre. To say that *shijo* appear inconclusive because they are not witty is to misread the facts completely. Wit is integral. Indeed it is the fusion of image and idea through wit, most often an ironical wit, that gives the *shijo* its unique flavor. This is evident in the four poems under discussion. Take the first poem:

> In this world medicine is plentiful
> and sharp knives abound, they say,
> but there's no knife to cut off affection, no medicine to forget true love.
> So be it:
> I'll leave my cutting and forgetting till I go to the other world.

Image and idea are fused in an ironical statement, which becomes clear only when one remembers that the traditional Confucian gentleman was not noted for his profound belief in the existence of an afterworld.

Now the second poem:

> Ride a horse through a field of flowers
> and the scent lingers on the hoof.
> Enter a wine-spring tavern and the smell of undrunk wine sticks fast.
> All we did
> was catch each other's eye; why then all the lies?

The opening and middle *chang* only hint at the context of this poem; the full statement of context is withheld until the final *chang*. The speaker comments on the social mores governing the boy-girl relationship in the society of the time and also on the universal tendency of people everywhere to engage in gossip. The irony in the poem consists in the fact that the boy and the girl are obviously attracted to each other, indicating that, after all, there is some fire causing all that smoke.

The third poem reads:

> My horse is neighing for the road,
> but my love won't let me go.
> The sun is crossing the mountain and I've a thousand *li* to go.
> Don't stop me,
> love, stop the setting sun.

Again, the mode of the poem is a witty ironical comment, which serves to unite the imagery in the earlier lines. The irony consists in the speaker's knowingly futile attempt to turn a beautiful moment into an eternal moment. At no time is there any hint that the speaker has lost his awareness of reality. In fact, the poem is a laughing comment on the futility of opposing time and fate.

Finally:

Look at that girl in blouse and patterned skirt,
her face prettily powdered, her hair as yet unpinned.
Yesterday she deceived me and now she's off to deceive another,
fresh-cut flowers
held firmly in her hand, hips swinging lightly as the sun goes down.

This poem, as already pointed out, is unusual in that the full statement of context is given in the middle *chang*. The final *chang* presents the girl's attitude toward society in addition to the poet's attitude toward the girl. The poet, in spite of his moral disapproval and his rueful feelings—this in itself is an irony—cannot hide a grudging admiration for the girl's beauty and her devil-may-care attitude to society at large. It is this complication of experience that gives the poem its punch.

The basic mode of the *shijo* is simplicity. In this it resembles all traditional Korean art forms, where the emphasis is not on decoration and elaboration but on simplicity and beauty of execution. There is something in the Korean sensibility that dislikes all unnecessary elaboration and decoration. This is fully reflected in the *shijo*, which relies heavily on simple images to achieve its effects. Examples abound:

Iced rice water
when merry with wine;
taking my lover in my arms again when he's about to leave at dawn.
What if others
discover these two great pleasures in life?

This is an intriguing poem. The sentiment expressed in the opening *chang* is something one would expect only a man to say, whereas that expressed in the middle *chang* seems to be spoken by a woman. Admittedly, the original text does not make this clear, but since it is invariably the man who is said to leave at dawn, it seems best to regard the speaker of the middle *chang* as a woman. If so, then the final *chang* would seem to be spoken by both in concert. The imagery in the poem is very effective. It is simple, direct, compressed, and it achieves its effect chiefly by contrast, the central contrast being between the exquisite coolness of the iced rice water and the heat of passionate love. The poem is pared down to the barest essentials. There is no elaboration, no decoration; it is as if the poet were almost at pains to avoid indirection. The conclusion effectively fuses image and idea through what is really a cliché. Everyone is aware of these great pleasures in life, but many people in their search for sophisticated pleasures tend to ignore the simple and beautiful. Obviously the mode here is once again that of ironical wit.

The following poem by Chŏng Ch'ŏl (1536–93) is another example of the simplicity, directness, and compression of *shijo* imagery:

> A shadow is reflected in the water:
> a monk is crossing the bridge.
> Monk, stay a moment; let me ask you where you're going.
> Stick pointed
> at the clouds, he passes without a backward glance.

A shadow—a monk crossing the bridge—the speaker asks a question—the monk answers with a gesture. On the surface the poem is simplicity itself, but in reality the experience is complex. The disparate experience of two men, a monk dedicated to attaining enlightenment and a speaker represented as indolent but ready to consider truth, is fused into something that in terms of meaning continues long past the last line of the poem. The poem is the expression of a personal revelation for the speaker. Ultimately the focus is on the speaker rather than on the monk. It is the speaker who is brought face to face with grinding truth; the monk presumably knows where life's path is leading him.

Take another example:

> How could the heart that loved the flower
> know that one day it would fall,
> or that love so sweet in candlelight would end in parting?
> Why is nature
> so unchanging while the human heart keeps changing day by day?

Once again, the imagery is simple: a flower—the flower falls—love—candlelight—parting; and the description is absolutely direct. The poem achieves its effect through contrast, or contradiction. In the opening *chang* the speaker refuses to acknowledge process as a part of nature, whereas in the final *chang* he describes nature as unchanging, the reference being, of course, to seasonal renewal, a favorite *shijo* theme that gives nature the appearance of being unchanging. Thus, the irony of the poem becomes apparent.

The mode of *shijo* is so simple and direct that a cursory reading might leave the reader with the impression that there is little metaphorical language in the form. This would be a misreading. There is plenty of metaphor in *shijo*, but its appearance can at times be subtle and may require a little digging. The type of metaphor in which two objects are explicitly compared is rather rare in *shijo*:

> Perhaps I am a magnet
> and girls are unthreaded needles.
> Sit down and they cling to me; stand up and they follow. Lie down
>     and they stick to me; bounce up and they don't fall off.
> Husbands and wives
> in marital disharmony, of magnet and needle compound a broth
>     and drink it twice a day.

The terms of the comparison in this poem by Kim Sujang (1690–?) are perfectly clear: the magnet represents the male, the needles unmarried girls, and the force of "unthreaded" should be quite clear. The final *chang* employs a conceit to point to the witty and ironical conclusion, a broth to create harmony from discord. The discord is literally that which occurs when the *kŏmun'go* and *pip'a*, two kinds of Korean lute, are not in tune. This type of metaphor explicitly identifying the two terms of the comparison is comparatively rare in *shijo*. One finds, very often, that only one term of the metaphor is explicitly identified. This is particularly true in the earlier *shijo*:

> White heron, do not go
> where crows squabble.
> Angry crows resent your whiteness.
> Clean now,
> washed in clear water, I fear your body may be sullied.

Chŏng Mongju's (1337–92) mother supposedly sang this song to warn her son against the dangers of Yi Sŏnggye's faction. General Yi Sŏnggye was the first king of the Chosŏn dynasty and Chŏng Mongju bitterly opposed the setting up of the new dynasty. The white heron is obviously Chŏng Mongju and the crows are partisans of Yi Sŏnggye. Take another example:

> White heron, do not mock
> the crow for being black.
> Black outside, is it black inside, too?
> White outside,
> black inside: that's really you.

Commentators note that this poem reflects the pangs of conscience felt by Yi Chik (1362–1431) for supporting the new Chosŏn dynasty. Against this background it becomes obvious that the white heron is a metaphor for the poet himself. In both these poems, the white heron also has symbolic connotations. The question of symbolism is treated below.

*Shijo* sometimes employ more subtle forms of metaphor, such as implied metaphor:

Candle, burning within the room,
from someone lately parted,
why are you unaware that inside you burn while outside you shed tears?
Ah candle,
you are so like me; you don't know your heart is burning up!

The word "tears" in this poem by Yi Kae (1417–56) is an implied metaphor in that the candle is likened to a person.

The conceit is another form of metaphor found in *shijo*:

Parting turns to fire;
it burns my innards up.
Tears become rain; perhaps they'll quench that fire.
But sighs
become the wind; will the fire live or die?

The development of the metaphor in this poem is based on cause and effect. Parting begets fire in the poet's heart; the pain of burning causes tears, which in turn become floods of rain, calculated whimsically as a possible way to put out the fire. However, tears are followed by sighs, which subsequently become the wind, and the poem ends with the dramatic "will the fire live or die?" The choice of imagery has obvious connotations. Fire, rain, and wind are among the most frightening images in nature, but the presumption is that just as fire, rain, and wind in nature run their course, so also the sorrow of parting will run its course. The speaker is at the moment inconsolable and, with poetic license, out of touch with reality.

There are a good many examples of *shijo* that develop a conceit along similar lines. They are always whimsical and humorous but somehow seem to fall short of the standards of the best *shijo* writing. However, there are some more deft examples of using the conceit for good poetic effect:

I'll cut a piece from the waist
of this interminable eleventh moon night,
and wind it in coils beneath these bed covers, warm and fragrant as the
spring breeze,

coil by coil
to unwind it the night my lover returns.

The effect of this poem by Hwang Chini (1502–?) is extremely subtle. A winter night is seen as unending, as are the coils that are to be cut from it. The metaphor is paradoxical and ironical, a section cut from the side of a personified interminable winter night, so long that it becomes synonymous with unending joy. As so often in the best *shijo*, contrast and irony combine to reveal a refined sensibility and a developed sense of wit. This is the *shijo* at its best, simple, direct, refined, witty.

In *shijo* poetry, metaphor and symbol are often combined, making it difficult to define the boundaries between the two. The difficulty is compounded by the fact that traditional commentators were quick to assign allegorical meanings to metaphors that otherwise might be taken as symbols. This occurs, for example, when metaphors such as "the great spreading pine" or "the sun" are taken as applying to historical personalities. This kind of interpretation results in a narrowing of the scope of *shijo* poetry.

Symbolism in *shijo* poetry draws heavily on the Chinese tradition. In terms of general background it may be useful to mention the system of Chinese cosmogony, which is known in Korean as the theory of *ohaeng*. Water, fire, wood, metal, and earth are the five basic elements. Earth and heaven combine to give birth to water in the north, fire in the south, wood in the east, metal in the west, and earth or clay in the center. This gives rise to the following relationships:

> north—water, winter, black, below, *hyonmu* (mythical animal)
> south—fire, summer, red, above, red sparrow
> east—wood, spring, blue, left, white tiger
> west—metal, autumn, white, right, blue dragon.

These relationships and associations, although not always applicable to specific poems, form a sort of general background to the imagery and symbolism in *shijo* poetry.

Another area of useful background information is the Korean (Chinese?) approach to color. Even a cursory examination of *shijo* reveals a preponderance of green, blue, and white: green pine, green bamboo, green waters, blue mountains, white heron, white gull. These colors seem to be associated with ideal man or man in an ideal state. Also, colors can have symbolic overtones quite familiar to readers of English poetry, for example, moonlight and whiteness together give an impression of isolation and loneliness. The question of color is complex and beyond the scope of this introduction. Suffice it to say that color often has symbolic overtones, and the reader should be aware of this in interpreting a particular poem.

*Shijo* poetry makes wide use of the conventional symbols of the Chinese tradition. These symbols are usually taken from nature—trees, flowers, and birds are particularly common. Examples of tree symbols would be pine and bamboo; green all the year around, they represent nobility of spirit, strength in adversity, and moral rectitude. Another example is the willow branch, a traditional symbol of parting. Flowers are symbolic of the passing of time, hence transience, the ephemeral, feminine beauty. Particular flowers are associated with particular qualities. A problem occurs here in crossing the double bridge of Chinese and Korean into English and finding suitable equivalents. For example, the plum in Yi Saek's poem (no. 8) is *maehwa* in Korean. Some dictionaries define the *maehwa* as the Japanese apricot or *ume*, but the word is usually translated into English as "plum." Korean commentators note that neither "apricot" nor "plum" is strictly accurate. At any rate, *maehwa* should not be confused with *ihwa*, which is also translated "plum" and has associations of changeableness or fickleness. *Maehwa* blooms in the frost; *ihwa* blooms in the spring. *Ihwa* occurs often in the company of *tohwa*, or peach, which is associated with ephemerality, feminine beauty, the frivolous. Korean switches very easily from tree to flower and vice versa, and often it is difficult to know which is meant. The chrysanthemum is usually associated with loyalty and nobility of spirit, but sometimes, too, it is used as a symbol of the transient, as in the line:

One touch of autumn frost and it becomes kindling for the fire.

Birds are also common conventional symbols. The cuckoo, for example, symbolizes unhappy love, from the legend of the Emperor of Shu, who fell in love with the wife of one of his ministers and metamorphosed into a cuckoo after death. The white gull is the friend of the simple man in nature; the magpie is the bearer of good news; the wild goose, usually though not always, symbolizes upright men or honest officials; and the crow corresponds to a corrupt official. Apart from birds, the only animals to occur regularly in *shijo* as conventional symbols are fish and the dog. The dog is a traditional sign of faithfulness, and the symbolism of fish varies from oppressed people to the bearers (carp) of good news. Horses and cattle occur

from time to time, but it is difficult to assign conventional symbolical mean-
ings to them. It is rather surprising that the tiger occurs so rarely in *shijo*,
but perhaps this is explained by the fact that the animals of *shijo*, by and large,
are the animals of the gentleman's garden or animals likely to be seen in
its environs.

These are just a sample of the conventional symbols that occur frequently.
It is by no means an exhaustive survey. However, what gives these symbols
their interest is the way in which the Korean poets took them and shaped
them to their own purposes, often using them in an ironical way. For exam-
ple, the pine tree is threatened by hostile forces, the cock and dog keep the
lover from coming, the black crow is dutiful to parents, the chrysanthemum
is kindling for the fire, the gull becomes black and the crow white, the wild
goose keeps the poet awake, the hunter shoots the wild goose, the fisherman
nets the carp. This sort of irony is at the heart of the *shijo* tradition, and it
goes a long way toward defining the Korean sensibility.

These are some of the ways in which metaphorical language is used in
*shijo*. The careful reader can discover many other examples. However, the
point is the mode of the *shijo*, and what has been said so far would seem to
bear out the judgment that the basic mode of the *shijo* is simplicity. The *shijo*
is a short song: the poet has just enough room to introduce an image, de-
velop it, and present a statement about his own experience. The very form of
the poem seems to militate against elaboration, decoration, and indirection.
There simply is no room for it. Even when metaphor is used, the *shijo* seems
to retain its simplicity and directness. However, it is interesting to note that
when the *sasŏl shijo* became popular in the eighteenth century, a distinct ten-
dency toward elaboration entered the form. Consider, for example, the fol-
lowing poem:

> Like a hen-pheasant chased by a hawk,
> without tree, rock, or stone for cover—
> Like a sailor on the high seas, a thousand bags of grain aboard, oars lost,
>     sails lost, rigging torn, mast broken, rudder gone, wind blowing, waves
>     breaking, shrouded in fog, day fading fast, ten thousand *li* to go,
>     darkness falling all around, the world a foaming, seething wave, and
>     now suddenly beset by pirates!
> Can this compare
> with how I felt when parting from my love two days ago?

The elaboration in this poem is effected by the simple expedient of compounding images. There is no question here of textual complexity or density. In fact, a reader whose starting point were not the classical *shijo* probably would not think in terms of elaboration or complexity in describing this poem. At the same time it must be admitted that the feeling engendered by this poem is quite different from that engendered by the classical form, and one way of accounting for this difference is in terms of elaboration.

The idea of professional poet was never part of the Korean tradition. The *shijo* poets of old Korea were, for the most part, refined and cultivated gentlemen, who savored the delights of composition in order to pass leisurely, convivial hours in the company of their friends. The composition of *shijo* was primarily a *yangban* (nobleman) accomplishment. It continued as such until the new generations of non-*yangban* singers, such as Kim Sujang in the eighteenth century and Pak Hyogwan and An Minyŏng in the nineteenth century, came to prominence under the influence of *Shirhak* (Practical Learning). Pak and An were, in fact, among the last of the great *shijo* poets. Subsequently, *shijo* went into decline.

To read *shijo* is to live and breathe the history and culture of Korea, to savor a tradition that is still alive and vibrant, with all the simple graces that have distinguished Korean art down through the centuries. *Shijo* are songs of the heart, without the artificiality and elaborate decoration that confuses rather than clarifies. *Shijo* are Korean, and they are Korea. Making the translations has been a labor of love.

# Texts and Sources

Han'guk shijo taesajŏn, edited by Pak Ŭlsu, published in 1991, is by far the most complete guide to shijo literature currently available. This two-volume book, beautifully produced, has texts, notes, classical allusions, and sources for 4,736 poems. The texts are arranged alphabetically.

Shijo munhak sajŏn, edited by Chong Pyŏng'uk, the old mainstay of shijo students, is still a very convenient collection of shijo for the non-Korean reader. It contains 2,376 poems, arranged alphabetically, and it provides sources, notes on difficult words and phrases, classical allusions, and information on poets. The major shortcoming of Shijo munhak sajŏn is that it is at least twenty years out of date in terms of texts and information on poets. In the past twenty years the canon of shijo has almost doubled.

Shim Chaewan's Yŏkdae shijo chŏnso has 3,335 poems, with all the variant readings, and his Shijoŭi munhonjok yŏn'gu is an exhaustive account of sources. However, Shim's books do not have allusions to classical sources nor do they have explanations of difficult words and phrases, although versions of the poems in modern han'gŭl script are provided.

The notes to the poems have been drawn from a number of sources. Apart from Pak, Chong, and Shim, extensive use has been made of Han'guk munhak chakkaron (1982) by So Chaeyong and others; Yokdae inmul han'guksa (1978), a work by numerous scholars coordinated and edited by the Han'guk ch'ulp'ansa yŏn'guso; Koshijo haesol (1982) co-authored by Yi T'aeguk and Han Ch'unp'yon; Koshijo non'go (1990) by Ch'oe Tongwon; and other general reference works.

The numbers indicating original texts refer to Shijo munhak sajŏn because it is the most convenient of the comprehensive anthologies to use and also because it is the anthology I used to do the translations. Texts differ from anthology to anthology. It seemed safer to give the text I used. It is a simple matter to proceed from any *chang* in the original Korean to the corresponding poem in the other anthologies. Where *Shijo munhak sajŏn* does not record a poem, the reference number, preceded by the word "Shim," is to *Yŏkdae shijo chŏnso*. The Yi Sebo poems were discovered after publication of the Chong and Shim volumes; the reference number to these poems, preceded by the word Pak, is to Pak Ŭlsu's *Han'guk shijo Taesajŏn*.

Poems with traditional ascriptions are arranged in chronological order. The anonymous poems are arranged in convenient categories: Moral Songs, Drinking Songs, Songs of Nature, Songs of Mortality, Love Songs, and Songs of Parting. These are thematic categories that commentators regularly use to discuss the poems. Inevitably there is some overlap. Opinions vary on where a particular song might be placed. The love category was so wide it seemed reasonable to divide the poems into Love Songs and Songs of Parting.

Romanization of *han'gŭl* is according to the McCune-Reischauer system. *Si*, however, is transcribed as *shi*: *shijo* and Shilla, for example, as opposed to *sijo* and Silla. The hyphen in Korean given names is dropped. An apostrophe is used to indicate syllable breaks when there is danger of confusion in pronunciation: for example Kwang'uk instead of Kwanguk. Pinyin is used to transcribe Chinese terms.

# PART I

*Songs from Koryŏ (918–1392)*

# PART I

# Songs from Koryŏ (918–1392)

## Ch'oe Ch'ung (984–1068)

Ch'oe Ch'ung was a Confucian scholar during the reign of Koryŏ king Munjong. Such was his fame that he was known as the Confucius of the East Sea. Pungmang Mountain in China was synonymous with the graveyard, death, or Hades.

1 (895)

> The searing sun sets on West Mountain;
> the Yellow River flows into the East Sea.
> Do the heroes of yesterday and today go in death to Pungmang
>     Mountain?
> So be it:
> all things wax and wane; is there any point in regret?

2 (1,735)
Fu Xi was a king in old China noted for the simplicity of his life.

> All my life I regret
> that I wasn't born in the time of Fu Xi.
> Though he wore grass clothes and ate berries,
> he retained
> the warmth of his disposition: this I shall envy always.

# Yi Kyubo (1168–1241)

Yi Kyubo, poet-bureaucrat, is the greatest of the *hanshi* (poems by Korean poets in Chinese characters) poets, a major poet by any standard. Although several thousand of his *hanshi* are extant, only one *shijo* poem seems to have survived.

3 (1,730)

> Warm weather, gentle breezes;
> birds twitter in song.
> I lie at leisure on a blanket of fallen leaves.
> Today
> my mountain home reposes in peace.

# U T'ak (1263–1342)

U T'ak was a scholar-official who retired early from the court because of palace scandals he uncovered in the course of his official duties. He devoted the rest of his life to scholarly pursuits.

4 (2,060)

> The breeze that melted the blue mountain snow
> blew suddenly and was gone.
> I'll borrow that breeze a moment and blow it across my head,
> to melt
> the frost lodged so long in these locks.

5 (2,270)

> In one hand I grasped a bramble,
> in the other I held a stick:
> the bramble to block the advance of age, the stick to stay approaching
>     white hair.
> White hair, though,
> outwitted me: it took a shortcut here.

## *Yi Cho'nyŏn (1269–1343)*

Yi Cho'nyŏn was a scholar-statesman who visited the Yuan court in Beijing several times as an envoy of the Koryŏ kings. This poem may have been written on one such visit. Composed almost entirely in Chinese characters, the poem presents some difficulty to the translator. The third line reads literally: "One branch (tree) spring heart how can the cuckoo know?" The description is highly symbolical and may refer to the poet's sweetheart, the king, or the country. Alternatively the poem may be taken as a sigh for the sad days that have come to the Koryŏ kingdom. In old Korea the night was divided into five watches, the third being the hour immediately before and after midnight.

6 (1,700)

> Moonlight white on white pear blossoms,
> the Milky Way in the Third Watch:
> how could the cuckoo know that spring suffuses the branch?
> Love, too,
> is like a sickness; I cannot sleep tonight.

## *Ch'oe Yŏng (1316–88)*

Ch'oe Yŏng was general of the army in the last days of Koryŏ. He had a brilliant military career, putting down several internal rebellions and repeatedly defeating invading Japanese pirates. In 1388 he was defeated in battle by his bitter rival Yi Sŏnggye, founder of the Chosŏn dynasty. Ch'oe was exiled and eventually killed. The song below reflects the courage, loyalty and indomitable will of the old warrior.

7 (516)

> Don't laugh at an old pine
> for bending under the weight of snow.
> Do spring breeze blossoms stay beautiful forever?
> When snowflakes
> fly in the wind, it's you who'll envy me.

## Yi Saek (1328–96)

Yi Saek was a scholar-official who was on friendly terms with Yi Sŏnggye and his group but refused to support the new dynasty. He was sent into exile after the murder of Chŏng Mongju. Yi Sŏnggye, recognizing his abilities, asked him to work for the new dynasty, but he refused. He expressed his disenchantment by retiring to the country, where he was known as Mogŭn or Hiding Cowherd. The plum is a traditional symbol of loyalty. The melting snow perhaps represents the waning Koryŏ dynasty threatened by hostile forces, which are symbolized here by the thick clouds. However, there is a diversity of opinion among scholars about the interpretation of the text. Not all agree that the snow is melting; some maintain that the verb modifier means "continuously falling"; others that it refers to a thick carpet of snow.

8 (890)

> Clouds cluster thick
> where white snow melts in the valley.
> The lovely plum, where has it bloomed?
> I stand alone
> in the setting sun, not knowing whither I should go.

## Yi Chik (1362–1431)

Yi Chik was one of the Koryŏ ministers who helped Yi Sŏnggye in the government of the new Chosŏn dynasty. He held a number of offices including that of prime minister. In the third year of the reign of T'aejong, he supervised the making of the first movable metal type. Some commentators point out that the poem below reflects his pangs of conscience for supporting Yi Sŏnggye.

9 (15)

> White heron, do not mock
> the crow for being black.
> Black outside, is it black inside, too?
> White outside,
> black inside: that's really you.

## Yi Pang'wŏn (T'aejong) (1367–1422)

Yi Pang'wŏn, the fifth son of General Yi Sŏnggye, was a pivotal figure in the plot to overthrow the Koryŏ dynasty and establish his father as the first king of the Chosŏn dynasty. Yi Pang'wŏn became the third king of the dynasty; he is known to history as T'aejong. While plotting to overthrow the Koryŏ dynasty, he gave a reception to which all the key political figures of the day were invited. Among them was Chŏng Mongju, a man renowned for his unshakable loyalty to the Koryŏ kings. Yi Pang'wŏn is said to have sung the following poem to Chŏng Mongju in order to observe the latter's reaction to a proffered alliance. Mansusan, literally "long-life-mountain," is outside the west gate of Songdo (Kaesŏng), the capital of Koryŏ. There are doubts about the authenticity of the ascription of the poem.

10 (1,641)

> What about living this way?
> What about living that way?
> What about arrowroot vines intertwining on Mansusan?
> Intertwined,
> we, too, could spend a hundred years in joy.

## Chŏng Mongju (1337–92)

Chŏng Mongju's response to the proposed alliance was unequivocal.

11 (1,666)

> Though my body die and die again,
> though it die a hundred deaths,
> my skeleton turn to dust, my soul exist or not,
> could the heart change
> that's red-blooded in undivided loyalty to its lord?

The poem is given added poignancy by the fact that supporters of Yi Pang'wŏn murdered Chŏng Mongju shortly thereafter. Tradition has it that Chŏng was aware of imminent death. Out of respect for his parents who had given him life, he thought it would be lacking in decorum to be other than drunk for the occasion. Accordingly, he consumed a large amount of wine before setting out to face death. Again tradition tells us that he mounted his horse back to front because he felt it would be unbecoming to see the fatal blow. Thus, he never saw the iron club that felled him as he crossed Sŏnjuk (Straight Bamboo) Bridge. A bamboo tree, a traditional symbol for unswerving moral probity, is said to have grown on the spot, and the stonework of the bridge is speckled red, which some like to regard as the blood of the hero. Again there is some doubt about the authenticity of the ascription of the poem.

## Chŏng Mongju's Mother

*Kagok wŏllyu* attributes this poem to Chŏng Mongju's mother, but the ascription is doubtful. There are two traditional interpretations of the poem. One sees it as a warning from a mother to her son, whom she sees destined for greatness, telling him to be careful how he comports himself. The second interprets the warning as more specific, namely, as referring to the famous banquet hosted by Yi Pang'wŏn. "Clear water" is a reference to a river in ancient China in which loyal ministers washed their ears whenever they were tempted by the lures of power and ambition.

12 (18)

> White heron, do not go
> where crows squabble.
> Angry crows resent your whiteness.
> Clean now,
> washed in clear water, I fear your body may be sullied.

## Yi Chono (1341–71)

Yi Chono was an official in the Koryŏ court who incurred the wrath of King Kongmin by writing a memorial to the throne deploring the violent acts of Shin Ton, a monk who was extremely powerful at court. Yi Chono escaped severe punishment through the intercession of Yi Saek. He was however, demoted, whereupon he retired and spent the rest of his life in seclusion. The clouds in the poem refer to the monk Shin Ton, who took advantage of the affection of King Kongmin to engage in corrupt practices, the point being that the clouds are responsible for their actions.

13 (224)

> To say that the clouds are unwitting
> is a groundless fabrication.
> High in the sky they ride, at liberty to go wherever they desire.
> Why on earth
> do they follow the sun and shade its dazzling light?

## Chŏng Tojŏn (?–1398)

Chŏng Tojŏn helped General Yi Sŏnggye found the Chosŏn dynasty; subsequently he rose to high office in the government. However, General Yi's son, Yi Pang'wŏn, killed him in a purge. Immortals' Bridge was in Songdo (Kaesŏng), the Koryŏ capital; Chahadong was a village nestling on the lower slopes of Songak (Pine Ridge) Mountain near Songdo.

14 (1,146)

> The water under Immortals' Bridge
> flows all the way to Chahadong,
> the sound all that remains of five hundred years of Koryŏ.
> Boy,
> there's no point in asking about the rise and fall of nations that are gone.

# PART II
# Chosŏn Dynasty: Foundation to the Hideyoshi War (1392–1592)

## PART II

# Chosŏn Dynasty: Foundation to the Hideyoshi War (1392–1592)

Some of the poets in this section were born during the Koryŏ period, but it seemed best to place them here because their poems, for the most part, reflect their attitude to the Chosŏn dynasty. Some chose to serve the new dynasty; others chose to remain faithful to Koryŏ.

## Cho Chun (1346–1405)

Cho Chun was one of the officials from the Koryŏ court who supported Yi Sŏnggye and the new Chosŏn dynasty. "Heaven my quilt, earth my pillow" is a quotation from Chinese poet Li Bai (701–62). Cho Chun's *shijo* are said to represent the pangs of conscience endured by the poet for not remaining loyal to the Koryŏ kings. The fisherman's pipe in the second poem may be the voice of conscience.

### 15 (1,258)

I drink till I'm drunk;
on the way home I sleep on the bare mountain.
Heaven my quilt, earth my pillow, who dares waken me?
A crazy wind
drives a fine rain and rouses me from sleep.

### 16 (1,133)

Fuddled with wine as the sun goes down,
loaded on the back of my donkey,
I pass, as in a dream, ten *li* through a mountain valley.
Somewhere
a bar on a fisherman's pipe wakens me from sleep.

## Kil Chae (1353–1419)

Kil Chae was one of the loyal scholar-officials at the end of the Koryŏ dynasty who opposed the emergence of the Chosŏn dynasty under Yi Sŏnggye. He spent the rest of his life in retirement, refusing all political preferment. He was known as Yaŭn, Hiding Blacksmith.

17 (1,501)

> Mounted on my horse, I visit
> Koryŏ's capital of five hundred years.
> Hills and streams are as they were, but great men are no more.
> Ah, yes,
> the glories of a golden age, were they only a dream?

## Maeng Sasŏng (1360–1438)

Maeng Sasŏng was a scholar-official who served both Koryŏ and Chosŏn. He had a reputation for moral probity and filial piety. Skilled in music as well as in poetry, he was a noted maker of musical instruments. Each of the poems in this series, which describes the four seasons on rivers and lakes, begins with the word *kangho*, a reference to a district in China with three rivers and five lakes found in a poem by Du Fu (712–70). *Kangho* may also be considered as describing the secluded world of a hermit. *Makkŏlli* is unrefined rice wine.

18 (100)

> Spring comes to rivers and lakes;
> I feel that crazy tingle.
> *Makkŏlli* to drink on the bank of the stream, the finest raw fish for
>     side dishes.
> Leisurely days,
> by the king's favor.

19 (97)

> Summer comes to rivers and lakes;
> there's nothing to be done under my grass roof.
> Gentle breezes propel trusty waves.
> Cool summer days,
> by the king's favor.

20 (95)

> Autumn comes to rivers and lakes;
> every fish is getting fat.
> I load the net in my tiny boat, cast it to the current's will.
> Restful days,
> by the king's favor.

21 (96)

> Winter comes to rivers and lakes;
> the snow is a foot deep.
> Rain hat slanted on my head; straw cape over my back.
> Days not cold,
> by the king's favor.

## Hwang Hŭi (1363–1452)

Hwang Hŭi had a long official career. He distinguished himself particularly during the reign of Sejong the Great. His songs are in the pastoral mode and reflect the great peace and prosperity of the period. "Rivers and lakes" in the first poem translates *kangho*, the district in China with three rivers and five lakes mentioned by Du Fu.

22 (101)

> Spring comes to rivers and lakes;
> there's a lot of work to be done.
> I mend the fishing net; the boy plows the field.
> When will we dig
> the medicinal roots sprouted on the mountain behind?

23 (636)

> Chestnuts are falling
> in the jujube red valley;
> crabs are crawling in the stubble.
> The wine is mature,
> the sieve peddler is on his rounds; what can I do but drink?

24 (2,042)

Why is spring so late
on blue stream banks outside my grass hut?
Willows are a lovely gold against the snow-white fragrance of pear.
Cuckoos singing
in the clouds of ten thousand peaks bring my heart the confusion
     of spring.

## Ha Wiji (1387–1456)

Ha Wiji was a high official in the Chosŏn government. His involvement
with Sŏng Sammun in the plot to restore Tanjong to the throne cost him
his life.

25 (110)

The guests have gone; the gate is closed;
the breeze has dropped; the moon is sinking low.
I open the wine jar again and recite a verse of poetry.
Perhaps this
is all the joy a recluse ever knows.

## Wŏn Ch'ŏnsŏk (1389–?)

When Yi Sŏnggye set up the new dynasty, Wŏn Ch'ŏnsŏk retired from his
official post. He spent the rest of his life farming, refusing a request from
T'aejong, whose tutor he had once been, to return to the court. The story is
told that he left six volumes of his writings, with instructions to his sons not
to open them. Disobeying their father's wishes, the sons opened the books
and discovered that they contained a compromising account of the fall of
Koryŏ. The sons burned the books for fear of possible repercussions. In the
first poem Wŏn Ch'ŏnsŏk expresses a mood of nostalgia and regret for the
glories of the Koryŏ dynasty. Manwŏl (Full Moon) Terrace refers to the site
of the Koryŏ royal palace in Songdo (Kaesŏng).

26 (2,371)

> The rise and fall of dynasties is in the hands of fate:
> Full Moon Terrace is overgrown with withered grass.
> The glories of five hundred years of Koryŏ meld in the herdsman's pipes.
> A traveler,
> passing in the setting sun, I cannot restrain my tears.

27 (515)

> Who says the bamboo bent in the snow
> has bowed down low?
> If it were its nature to bow, would it be green in the snow.
> It seems to me
> you alone stand loyal against winter's worst!

## Kim Chongsŏ (1390–1453)

Kim Chongsŏ was a general who distinguished himself during the reign of Sejong by driving back invaders from the Manchurian border. He also served with distinction under Munjong and Tanjong. However, Prince Suyang, the future King Sejo, had the general and his two sons assassinated as part of his campaign to wrest the throne from Tanjong.

28 (1,036) Song of the Hero's Spirit

> North wind bitter through the branches,
> bright moon frigid in the snow,
> great-sword drawn, I stand in this remote border fortress.
> Long whistle,
> mighty shout; nothing dares oppose me.

## Yi Kae (1417–56)

Yi Kae was one of the Six Martyred Subjects who lost their lives as a result of the plot to restore the boy king Tanjong to the throne. The poem refers to Tanjong's banishment to Yŏngwŏl, a remote valley in Kangwŏn Province. The image of the candle shedding tears occurs frequently in classical Chinese poetry.

29 (865)

> Candle, burning within the room,
> from someone lately parted,
> why are you unaware that inside you burn while outside you shed tears?
> Ah candle,
> you are so like me; you don't know your heart is burning up!

## Pak P'aengnyŏn (1417–56)

Pak P'aengnyŏn was one of the Six Martyred Subjects implicated in the plot to restore Tanjong to the throne. While Pak was in jail, Sejo is supposed to have sent the spy Kim Chil to see him. Kim Chil was instructed to recite the poem Yi Pang'wŏn had once recited to Chŏng Mongju (see no. 10, p. 31) and to observe Pak's reaction. The following *shijo* was his answer. The characters translated as "bright moon" literally refer to two precious stones, *yagwang* and *myŏngwŏl*, the former meaning "bright at night," and the latter "bright moon." *Yagwangmyŏngwŏl* represents Tanjong, and the crow represents Sejo.

The second poem is a further expression of the poet's loyalty. "Lishui," translated as "fair waters," refers to a place in China. "Kunkang," translated as mountains, is another name for Kunlun shan in China.

30 (17)

> A crow in sleet appears white
> but soon turns black again.
> Could the bright moon be dark at night,
> or the heart change
> that's red-blooded in undivided loyalty to its lord?

31 (287)

> Because gold is found in fair waters,
> does all water have gold?
> Because jade is found in the mountains, does every mountain have jade?
> Important
> though love may be, must one follow a host of lovers around?

## Sŏng Sammun (1418–56)

Sŏng Sammun was one of the Six Martyred Subjects implicated in the plot to overthrow Sejo and restore Tanjong to the throne. The following poem is said to have been sung after the plot had failed and Sŏng Sammun was awaiting execution. Pongnaesan was one of the mountains in China where the Immortals dwelt; here it is used as the summer name for the Diamond Mountains. The pine is a traditional symbol of unswerving loyalty.

32 (1,665)

> What will I be, you ask,
> when my body is dead and gone?
> On the topmost peak of Pongnaesan a great spreading pine is what I'll be,
> there to stand
> lone and green when snow fills all heaven and earth.

## Yu Ŭngbu (?–1456)

Yu Ŭngbu was one of the Six Martyred Subjects implicated in the plot to assassinate Sejo and restore Tanjong to the throne. As a military officer, Yu was entrusted with the task of striking the fatal blow against Sejo at a banquet for a Ming envoy. Kim Chil betrayed the plot to the king. Yu Ŭngbu was arrested, tortured, and executed. The snow and frost reflect the cruelty of Sejo, the pines represent the men of rank, and the flowers are the young men of talent who have yet to make their reputation in the political sphere. The poem refers to the innocent blood spilled by Sejo in the course of usurping the throne.

33 (61)

> The wind that blew last night
> brought snow and frost,
> and the great spreading pines have all fallen to the ground.
> No need to speak
> the fate of flowers yet to bloom.

34 (1,455)

> Did the wind that blew two days ago
> blow also on rivers and lakes?
> How did the boatmen who crowd the river fare?
> I've been so long
> in mountains and forests, I fear I have no news of the world.

## *Yu Sŏng'wŏn (?–1456)*

Yu Sŏng'wŏn was one of the Six Martyred Subjects involved in the plot to overthrow Sejo and restore Tanjong to the throne. When he got the news that the plot had failed, he returned home, drank some wine with his wife, and took his own life in front of the shrine housing his ancestral tablets. The poem refers to the death of Kim Chongsŏ by order of Sejo, at that time Prince Suyang. The murder was one step on Sejo's route to the usurpation of power. The fisherman's song is variously regarded as the news of Kim's death or as a symbol of the struggle for power that characterized the era. The age of great peace refers to the reign of Sejong. The *kŏmun'go* is a traditional Korean stringed instrument.

35 (2,110)

> Lying at leisure under my grass roof,
> my head cradled on the *kŏmun'go*,
> I sought in dreams at least to see a reign of great peace,
> but the fisherman's song
> piped at the gate awakened me from sleep.

## *Tanjong (1441–57)*

Grandson of Sejong the Great, Tanjong became the sixth king of the dynasty. However, Prince Suyang, the future King Sejo, usurped the boy king's throne and sent him in exile to Yŏngwŏl, a beautiful valley in Kangwŏn Province. Tanjong was subsequently poisoned at Sejo's orders. The poem, written mostly in Chinese, scarcely has the *shijo* form at all. However, the beauty of the language and the intimations of approaching death combine to give it a memorable quality. The cuckoo is a traditional symbol of unhappy love.

36 (2,128)

> The cuckoo calls; the moon is low on the mountain;
> I lean against this balustrade thinking of distant friends.
> The anguish in your voice suffuses my heart. Were you silent, I would
>   not be sad.
> To friends from whom I have parted, I say:
> do not come here in spring when the cuckoo calls and the moon is bright
>   on the pavilion.

## Kim Koengp'il (1454–1504)

Kim Koengp'il was a scholar celebrated for his filial piety. Known as one of the five wise men of Chosŏn, he lost his life in one of the many purges that characterized the era. The poem is sometimes attributed to Maeng Sasŏng.

37 (1,082)

> Clad in rain hat and straw rain gear,
> I shoulder my hoe in the fine rain.
> I weed the mountain field, lie down in green shade.
> Herdboys
> driving cattle home waken me from sleep.

## Wang Pang'yŏn (fifteenth century)

No precise dates are available for Wang Pang'yŏn. We know, however, that he was a court official and that he escorted Tanjong into exile in Yŏng'wŏl. He also accompanied the royal messenger one year later who brought the poison that the boy king had been sentenced to drink. The poem refers to Wang's feelings after escorting Tanjong to Yŏng'wŏl.

38 (1,987)

> I parted from my fair lord
> in a spot ten million *li* away.
> With nowhere to entrust my heart, I sit on the bank of the stream.
> The water
> is like my heart; it cries as it travels the night.

## Wŏn Ho (fifteenth century)

No dates are available for Wŏn Ho. However, we know that he resigned his official post when Sejo usurped the throne and that he followed Tanjong to Yŏngwŏl, where he lived in an old hermitage. When sadness became unbearable, tradition says he used to face in the direction of Tanjong's abode and shed tears.

### 39 (63)

> The stream that wept last night
> wept plaintively and passed.
> It seems to me now that it brought the tears of my lord.
> If the current
> reversed itself, I too would send my tears.

## Prince Wŏlsan (1454–88)

Prince Wŏlsan was the grandson of Sejo and the elder brother of Sŏngjong. He seems to have had more taste for art than for political affairs and to have spent his life accordingly. The poem is actually a free translation of a Chinese poem, *Chuan zi he shang shi*.

### 40 (2,136)

> Autumn night falls on the river;
> the water grows chill.
> I cast a line, but the fish do not bite.
> Loaded only
> with insensible moonlight, I row back an empty boat.

## Yi Hyŏnbo (1467–1555)

Yi Hyŏnbo was a scholar-official who got into trouble during the reign of Yŏnsan'gun because he exposed the misdeeds of a number of royal secretaries. He was sent into exile for his pains. In 1505 he was restored to favor and afterward had a distinguished career in the public service. He requested retirement several times. Finally when permission was still not forthcoming, he downed tools and went home. His poems are filled with a sense of the peace and harmony of a simple life in nature in contrast to the rough and tumble of public life. The first four poems are from *Songs of a Fisherman*.

41 (2,104)

> Rice wrapped in a green lotus leaf,
> the day's catch strung on a willow branch,
> I moor my boat among the rushes.
> Who can know
> the simple freshness of the taste?

42 (1,040)

> Leisurely clouds stand on the mountaintop;
> white gulls fly in the water;
> two sights that unwittingly gladden the heart.
> I'll forget
> the troubles of this life and frolic with you both.

43 (226)

Red dust traditionally refers to the cares of public life.

> Look down: deep green waters.
> Look around: ten thousand blue mountain folds.
> How the scene conceals the red dust of the world!
> And when the moon
> shines white on the water, I'm even more abstracted.

44 (1,635)

> Thus I have no worries;
> I live a fisherman's life.
> Floating my tiny boat on waves that never end,
> oblivious
> of the affairs of men, how can I feel the passing of the days?

45 (501) Song of Nongam

Nongam Rock was in Yi Hyŏnbo's hometown in Kyŏngsang Province. He wrote this poem after retiring from the public service.

> Up on top of Nongam Rock
> an old man's eyes become bright and clear.
> The affairs of men may change, but can mountains and streams depart?
> The water and hills
> fronting this rock are as I saw them yesterday.

46 (1,495)

"Rivers and lakes" once again translates the term *kangho*, a reference to a region in China with three rivers and five lakes, mentioned in a poem by Du Fu, with the secondary meaning of the abode of a hermit.

> Desultory rain falls on the paulownia tree;
> the autumn breeze blows briefly.
> My heart is filled with care; why do the cicadas cry?
> The wild goose,
> perhaps, has news of rivers and lakes.

47 (188)

> Are there limits to man's desire for fame and honor?
> Long life and early death are in the hands of Heaven.
> Though girded with a gold-embroidered belt, how many springs can a
>     bent old man hope to greet?
> Days like today
> are by the king's favor.

## Chŏng Hŭiryang (1469–?)

Chŏng Hŭiryang was an official in the court of Yŏnsan'gun. He was exiled by the king for failing to report the Muosahwa Incident, a factional fight in 1498.

48 (2,369)

> Don't go into the water first
> saying flowing streams run shallow.
> Don't travel abroad saying the setting sun is still high.
> Give fewer assurances
> to me, my friend, and take more care yourself.

## Kim Ku (1488–1534)

Kim Ku, an official during the reign of Chungjong, was one of the outstanding calligraphers of his day. In 1519, while serving in the Royal Archives, he became involved in the introduction of a new political ideology, for which he was duly arrested and sent into exile. Returning from exile years later, he grieved so much at his parents' tomb, we are told, that the grass around the grave withered, and Kim himself fell ill from grief and died.

One moonlit night King Chungjong heard Kim Ku reading aloud. The king was so impressed by the beauty of Kim's reading that he requested the poet to compose a song. The following is one of the two poems composed in answer to the king's request.

49 (1,538)

> Till the wild duck
> grows legs like the crane,
> till the black crow becomes the white heron,
> even so long,
> may you enjoy happiness, good health, and long years.

50 (1,046)

The peach is associated with ephemeral beauty, fickleness, and the exotic. Red, pink, and white are the colors of the three-colored variety.

> I spy the three-colored peach blossom
> floating down the mountain stream.
> A free spirit, I jump in, fully clothed.
> Flowers scooped
> in my arms, I splash up and down in the water.

51 (2,196)

> Mountains may be high,
> but they are beneath heaven.
> Waters may be deep, but they are above the earth.
> The king's favor
> is what's truly high and truly deep.

## Sŏ Kyŏngdŏk (1489–1546)

Sŏ Kyŏngdŏk was a Confucian scholar who devoted his life to scholarly pursuits in the seclusion of his mountain retreat near Songdo (Kaesŏng). Hwang Chini, the legendary *kisaeng*, was one of his students, and tradition has it that the old Confucian master loved her dearly. The lady in the first of the two *shijo* below is said to be Hwang Chini. In the second poem "I" may refer to Sŏ Kyŏngdŏk in his role as Confucian scholar, and "you" may refer to Hwang Chini.

52 (713)

> I'm a fool at heart
> and everything I do is foolish.
> It's too much to expect my love to come to this cloudy mountain valley,
> yet the sound
> of leaves falling in the breeze makes me wonder is it she?

53 (712)

> Heart, what is the secret
> of your continuing youth?
> When I grow old, can you avoid growing old, too?
> I fear
> people will laugh at me for following you around.

## Song Sun (1493–1583)

Song Sun was a scholar-official during the reign of Myŏngjong. In old age he retired from public life, built a retreat in the mountains near Tamyang in South Chŏlla and devoted himself to literary pursuits. The story is told that Myŏngjong sent a bunch of newly blossomed chrysanthemums to the Jade Hall, another name for Hongmungwan, the Royal Archives, and requested a suitable poem on the subject. Since none of the officials could come up with a poem, they requested Song Sun to answer the challenge. Song Sun in his poem interpreted the king's action as a request to the officials to be loyal like the chrysanthemum rather than fickle and changeable like spring blossoms. The ascription of the poem is not quite certain; several collections attribute it to Chŏng Ch'ŏl.

54 (1,091)

> With yellow chrysanthemums newly bloomed
> on this day of compounded wind and frost,
> My Lord fills the golden bowl and sends it to the Jade Hall.
> Peach and plum,
> don't pretend to be flowers; I know the mind of My Lord.

55 (1,309)

> Ten years I've striven
> to build this three-room straw hut:
> one room for me, one for the moon, and one for the fresh breeze.

No place for
mountains and streams; I'll put them all around me and view them there.

## An Chŏng (1494–?)

An Chŏng was a county chief during the reign of Chungjong. He was skilled in calligraphy and in paintings of the four glorious gentlemen—plum, bamboo, orchid, and chrysanthemum.

56 (1,863)

As I ride along on my lame donkey,
the sun sets on west mountain.
When mountain trails are rough, can rock streams flow gently?
I hear a dog
bark on the wind; I think I must be near.

## Sŏng Un (1497–1579)

Sŏng Un had a short career in public service. He retired to the country during one of the purges and stayed there for the rest of his life. He was promoted posthumously.

57 (1,829)

Spring comes to the countryside;
I have a lot to do.
Who will transplant the flowering trees? When will the medicine patch
   get plowed?
Boy,
cut me some bamboo; I'll make a rain hat first.

## Yi Hwang (1501–70)

Yi Hwang, better known by his pen name T'oegye, was born in Andong. He distinguished himself by his scholarship and was appointed minister of ceremonials by Sŏnjo. However, he had great difficulty coping with the factional infighting that was a feature of the period. This combined with a delicate constitution forced him on a number of occasions to retire from the rigors of public life to the tranquility of his mountain retreat, Tosan. In Tosan he founded a *sŏdang*, or school, and won a reputation for himself as Korea's greatest philosopher.

Yi Hwang's *shijo* reflect the Confucian bent of his mind. *Twelve Songs of Tosan* is a summary of the Confucian way. The poems counsel a life devoted to personal cultivation in harmony with the rhythms of nature. The message may have little appeal to the modern reader, but Yi Hwang's love of nature and his delight in whimsy are at the center of the tradition of *shijo* poetry.

## Twelve Songs of Tosan

*First Series*

58 (1,640) 1

> What about living this way?
> What about living that way?
> What matter how a country buff lives?
> Why try to cure
> the incurable: my longing for rocks and springs?

59 (1,477) 2

> Twilight haze is my home;
> wind and moon are my friends.
> In an age of peace I sicken into old age.
> In all this
> I have but one wish: to be free from fault.

60 (1,237) 3

> To say simplicity is dead
> is certainly a lie.
> To say the human spirit is noble is certainly the truth.
> Is it possible
> to deceive so many talented men under Heaven?

61 (1,616) 4

> There are fragrant orchids in the valley;
> nature is sweet to the ear.
> There are white clouds on the mountain; nature is sweet to the eye.
> In all this,
> I cannot forget my beautiful lord?

62 (1,053) 5

The white colt was the traditional mount of the wise man or the victor in ancient China. The reference here seems to be to the continuing ambition of the young men under Yi Hwang's tutelage.

There's a terrace in front of the mountain;
beneath the terrace a flowing stream.
A flock of gulls flies to and fro.
Why does
the sage's white colt set its heart so far away?

63 (2,159) 6

Spring breezes fill the mountains with flowers;
autumn night floods the terrace with moonlight.
The joys of the four seasons are like man himself.
Need I add:
fish jump, hawks soar; the sky is filled with shade and light. Can all
    this come to an end?

*Second Series*

64 (1,999) 1

I return to Sky-cloud Terrace;
my study is bright and clean.
There's no end to the pleasures of a life with ten thousand books.
In all this,
there's no need to tell the delights of leisurely walks.

65 (503) 2

Though thunder topple the mountains,
a deaf man cannot hear.
Though the sun climb to the center of the heavens, a blind man
    cannot see.
We who are
sharp-eared and bright-eyed, let's not be like the deaf and blind.

66 (145) 3

> The ancients cannot see me;
> I cannot see the ancients.
> Though I cannot see the ancients, the road they've walked lies before me.
> With the road
> they've walked before me, how can I avoid walking it?

67 (612) 4

> The road I once walked
> I abandoned for several years.
> I traveled here and there and have but lately returned.
> Now that I'm back,
> I'll never let my heart wander again.

68 (2,065) 5

> Why are green mountains
> eternally green?
> Why do flowing waters keep flowing night and day?
> We, too,
> will never cease to be eternally green.

69 (1,578) 6

> Even ignorant men seek perfection;
> perhaps the way is easy.
> Not even wise men can be perfect; perhaps the way is difficult.
> Easy or difficult,
> between the two, I do not feel the advance of age.

## Cho Shik (1501–72)

Cho Shik was a celebrated neo-Confucian scholar. Although recommended for public office by Yi Hwang and others, he refused all offers of appointment. Deploring the weakening moral values of the times, he retired to Chirisan, a mountain in the southern provinces, where he devoted himself to training his students.

70 (686)

> I'd heard of Chirisan's meeting of the waters,
> now I see it for myself.
> The shadow of the mountain is immersed in clear water where peach
> blossoms float.
> Boy,
> where is the other world; might this be it here?

71 (1,450)

> Dressed in hemp through the worst of winter,
> exposed to rain and snow in this rock-hole hut,
> I've never basked in the rays of a cloud-screened sun,
> yet when I hear
> that the sun has crossed west mountain, I cannot restrain my tears.

## Hwang Chini (1502–?)

A special mystique surrounds the name of Hwang Chini, the celebrated *kisaeng*-poet of the sixteenth century. A member of a despised class, a registered *kisaeng*, she not only associated freely with aristocrats, scholars, and artists but defied all the accepted conventions of the time. She is said to have detested pomposity and never to have given her favor to a man who did not appreciate good wine, good music, and good poetry. Most of the *shijo* attributed to her deal with aspects of the theme of love.

72 (672)

> I'll cut a piece from the waist
> of this interminable eleventh moon night,
> and wind it in coils beneath these bed covers, warm and fragrant as the
> spring breeze,
> coil by coil
> to unwind it the night my lover returns.

73 (1,427)

> Ah, what have I done?
> Did I not know I'd miss him so?
> Had I bid him stay, would he have gone?
> But I did it;
> I sent him away, and I can't tell you how I miss him.

74 (434)

> When was I faithless,
> when did I ever deceive my love?
> The dark moonless night runs late, and still there's not a sign of him.
> Leaves falling
> in the autumn breeze, what can I do?

75 (1,050)
When Sŏ Kyŏngdŏk died, Hwang Chini wrote this poem in tribute to her old teacher.

> The mountains are ancient,
> not so the waters.
> Water flowing night and day, how can it be the same?
> Great men
> are like that water; they go but do not return.

76 (2,056)
A Confucian worthy, Pyŏkkyesu (Blue Stream), on a visit to Songdo (Kaesŏng) boasted that he was impervious to the charms of any woman. Chini (Bright Moon) challenged him with this provocative poem.

> Blue Stream, do not boast
> of swift passage through green mountains,
> for having reached the sea, the return trip assumes real difficulty.
> Bright Moon fills
> the empty mountain; why not rest a little here?

## Kim Inhu (1510–60)

Kim Inhu was an official during the turbulent reign of Myŏngjong. Incidents such as the one that forms the background to this poem were common at the time. Criticism of the conduct of the queen mother and some evil retainers led to a series of arrests, banishments, and executions. Im Hyŏngsu was one of those executed, and Kim Inhu's poem deplores his death. In fact, Kim Inhu became so disgusted with the factional fighting in the court that he quit his official position and devoted himself to scholarly pursuits. There is a dispute about the authorship of the poem: Kogŭm kagok ascribes it to Chŏng Ch'ŏl. However, most scholars feel that the background to the poem makes Kim Inhu the likely author. The Great Hall refers to the seat of government, presumably the Royal Palace.

77 (1,393)

> Ah, they're cutting it down;
> they're cutting down the great spreading pine.
> Had it been left a while, it might have become a center beam.
> If the Great Hall
> totters, with what shall it be buttressed?

78 (2,055)

> Blue mountains go their way;
> green waters go their way.
> Mountains their way, waters their way, and me my way among them.
> I've grown my way
> among them; among them my way I'll grow old.

## Yu Hŭich'un (1513–77)

Yu Hŭich'un was a scholar-bureaucrat who served under Chungjong and Sŏnjo. In 1547 he became embroiled in a political squabble and was exiled to Cheju Island. However, in 1567 he was released and recalled to service. The following poem is said to have been written while Yu Hŭich'un was stationed in Wansan, to mark the visit of the royal messenger, Pak Sun.

79 (816)

> I've dug and washed
> this bunch of parsley:
> to My Lord I offer it, to My Lord alone.
> The flavor
> is nothing special; taste again and see.

## Song In (1516–84)

Song In married the daughter of a concubine of Chungjong and held various official positions in court. He was a man of noted personal refinement, respected by Yi Hwang, Yi Yulgok, and other prominent men of the time. Like many of the great Confucian scholars, he delights in singing the pleasures of the drinking cup.

80 (2,258)

Thirty days in the month
without leaving the wine cup down.
No pain in my arm, no blisters on my lips.
Why get sober
when every day is pain free?

81 (698)

I forget as soon as I hear;
what I've seen is as unseen.
My approach to affairs being thus, I am ignorant of the rights and wrongs
    of men.
All I know
is that my hand is whole: I'll use it to hold the cup.

## Yang Saŏn (1517–84)

Yang Saŏn was a scholar-official during the reign of Myŏngjong. He loved to
travel by palanquin through the Diamond Mountains, giving himself up to
the beauty of nature. He is famous for carving a *paduk* (Go) board on a huge
rock in the Diamond Mountains and inscribing the following Chinese poem
on it: "Pongnae Maple Rock: On Wings Climb to Heaven."

82 (2,195)

The mountain may be high,
    but it is still below heaven.
Climb and climb again; everyone can reach the summit.
Only he
who never climbs insists the mountain is high.

## Yang Ŭngjŏng (1519–?)

Yang Ŭngjŏng served as an official under Chungjong and Myŏngjong. He
was noted for his skill in poetry.

83 (2,202)

Peace in heaven and on earth:
lunchbox and gourd I sling across my shoulder.
My sleeves are down, rippling in rhythm, to show

my joy
at being untrammeled by the world.

## Yi Hubaek (1520–78)

Yi Hubaek was a scholar-official who served with distinction during the reigns of Chungjong and Sŏnjo. His proficiency in literature was evident from the first and he quickly built himself a considerable reputation.

84 (1,520)

> A plum branch lay
> abandoned by the road.
> I picked it up and planted it in a pot.
> Already
> it is the twelfth moon: the plum has bloomed, but its master I do
>     not know.

85 (2,140)

> Wild goose, alarmed by autumn frost,
> give up your senseless crying.
> Here I am in a strange land, separated from my love.
> With you crying
> in the night, I can't get any sleep.

86 (2,213)

> Wild geese light on the broad sweep of sand;
> the sun sets on the river village.
> Nights when the fishing boats are already home and the white gulls
>     are asleep,
> somewhere,
> a few long-drawn bars on the flute waken me from sleep.

## Kang Ik (1523–?)

Kang Ik was an official during the reign of Chungjong. He devoted himself so completely to reading and writing that he never got much promotion in the bureaucracy.

87 (1,282)

> The dog barks at the brushwood gate:
> who could it be in this mountain village?
> Ah, it's just spring birds singing in the green of the bamboo grove.
> Boy,
> if anyone comes for me, say I've gone to dig fernbrake.

## Kim Sŏng'wŏn (1525–97)

Kim Sŏng'wŏn was a scholar who liked to engage in poetry contests with famous poets of the time. During the Hideyoshi War he was caught and slain by the Japanese while attempting to flee to safety with his mother.

88 (468)

> Drifting clouds to vent their spleen
> hide the bright moon's light.
> Endless longing fills my heart as I sit alone throughout the night.
> The wind,
> aware of my feelings, drives the rain to me.

## Kwŏn Homun (1532–87)

Kwŏn Homun passed the civil service examination when he was thirty. Shortly thereafter, his parents died, whereupon he resigned his position and spent the next six years mourning. He built a study beneath Ch'ŏngsŏng Mountain and devoted himself to literary pursuits. As his reputation grew, more and more scholars and literary men frequented his house. His *shijo* sing the simple joys of country life. The poet's starting point seems to be an overpowering awareness of the transience of human existence and the consequent futility of being concerned with power and material goods. Hence, the wise man lives in nature. However, having to refuse repeated requests from the king to assume public office caused the poet some inner conflict.

89 (78)

> I lie on the bank of the river
> watching the water flow by.
> Times flows like that; a hundred years slip by in a moment.
> The ambition
> of ten years melts away like ice.

The following are from *Eighteen Songs of Leisure.*

90 (94)

> Diverting oneself on rivers and lakes
> means abandoning a wise king.
> Serving a wise king conflicts with the pleasant things in life.
> I stand alone
> at the fork, not knowing whither I should go.

91 (370)

> At the end of the day
> there's no more work to be done.
> I close the pine-branch gate and stretch beneath the moon,
> without a
> follicle of interest in the affairs of men.

92 (1,842)

> Nights after rain when the moon
> cuts through the clouds to land on pine branch tips,
> slanting brilliant light across the blue stream,
> seagulls
> in a flock follow me around.

93 (1,379)

> The rain clears over the fishing hole:
> green moss I throw like stones in the water.
> I count the fish! How I wish I could catch some!
> The crescent moon
> is a silver hook immersed in the heart of the blue stream.

94 (834)

> Breeze ever fresh,
> moon ever bright,
> not a mote of dust in bamboo grove or pine pavilion.
> The *kŏmun'go*
> and ten thousand books make for even finer feelings.

95 (1,603)

> I come to a deserted pavilion;
> moonlight and tinkling stream commingle.
> I train my eyes on the moonlight, my ears on the stream.
> I listen, I look:
> the world is a harmony of brightness.

96 (1,898)

> The pursuit of wine and women
> is not for the poet.
> The search for riches and honors is not for me.
> So be it:
> fisherman-shepherd is the job for me; I'll divert myself on the banks of a
>     solitary stream.

## Yi Yangwŏn (1533–92)

Yi Yangwŏn fought bravely during the Hideyoshi War and was promoted to prime minister. The Japanese attacked again, and a rumor circulated that the king had fled to Manchuria. Grieving at the news, Yi Yangwŏn fasted for eight days, hemorrhaged, and died. The poem satirizes those who plot treason, the lofty tree being an allusion to the office of prime minister.

97 (479)

> I'm up in this lofty tree
> because you put me there.
> Look here, my friends, stop shaking the trunk.
> If I fall and die,
> that's no great sadness; my fear is I won't be able to see my lord.

## Yu Chashin (1533–1612)

Yu Chashin was the father-in-law of Kwanghaegun. He served as minister of justice.

98 (2,138)

> Autumn mountains tinted in the fading light
> are immersed in the heart of the river.
> Bamboo rod in hand I sit in my tiny boat,

the world so much
at leisure, the lord of heaven sends the moon along.

## Sŏng Hon (1535–98)

Sŏng Hon was a prominent neo-Confucian scholar during the reign of
Sŏnjo. He made a spirited defense of his friend Yi Yulgok when the latter
was accused of treason.

99 (733)

> Wordless the blue mountains,
> formless the flowing waters;
> priceless the fresh breeze, ownerless the bright moon.
> Amid all this,
> free of sickness, I shall grow gracefully old.

## Yi I (1536–84)

Yi I, better known by his pen name Yulgok, was one of Korea's greatest
Confucian scholars. The Kosan series of ten poems, written in old age, when
Yulgok was engrossed in study and teaching, is modeled on a series by Zhu
Xi, *Nine Songs of Wuyi Mountain*.

### Nine Scenic Glories of Kosan

100 (142)

> The nine scenic glories of Kosan
> are unknown in the world of men.
> From grass I've cut I weave my hut: friends all come to visit.
> In imagination
> I'm on Wuyi Mountain, studying Zhu Xi.

101 (1,729)

> First is
> the sun lighting Crown Rock.
> Mist lifts from verdant fields: far and near are painted scenes.
> The green wine jar
> I set among the pines, and I watch the approach of friends.

102 (1,633)

> Second is
> spring coming late to Flower Rock.
> I float petals down green waters, sending them to distant fields.
> The world knows
> nothing of this lovely place: I think I shall be beauty's herald.

103 (1,070)

> Third is
> green foliage spread across Kingfisher Screen.
> When mountain birds sing high and low on green waters,
> balmy breezes
> blow through stunted pines: summer disappears.

104 (993)

> Fourth is
> the sun crossing Pine Cliff.
> Rocks shadowed in the water reflect a myriad colors.
> Woods and springs,
> the deeper, the better: I cannot contain the tingle I feel.

105 (1,484)

> Fifth is
> Secluded Screen: what a lovely sight!
> My riverside retreat is cool and clean.
> Amid all this
> I'll study and teach; I'll sing the wind, recite the moon.

106 (1,624)

> Sixth is
> the broad expanse of water at Fish Point.
> Who has the greater joy, the fish or me? I do not know.
> In fading light
> I shoulder my fishing pole: the moon illumines the pathway home.

107 (2,173)

> Seventh is
> autumn colors on Maple Rock.
> A light frost turns the cliff to embroidered silk.

I sit alone
on the chill rock and forget all about home.

108 (2,207)

Eighth is
bright moonlight on *Kŏmun'go* Creek.
I play three or four tunes on a fine jade instrument.
Who knows
these old tunes? I play for personal pleasure.

109 (216)

Ninth is
the winter sun setting on Mun Mountain.
Weird rocks and fantastic stones are buried in the snow.
Sightseers
do not come: they say there's nothing to see.

## Chŏng Ch'ŏl (1536–93)

Royal inspector, governor of a province, personal secretary to the king, second prime minister, general of the army—these are some of the positions held by Chŏng Ch'ŏl during a career that was punctuated by periods of voluntary retirement, dismissal, and exile. He was by nature a brilliant but rather stubborn man, and his career is marked by continuous controversy. Chŏng Ch'ŏl is a poet of the first rank, indeed the first *shijo* poet to leave to posterity a considerable body of poems, 107 to be exact. These poems reveal the startling phrase, the spare, elegant expression, the density of meaning, the telling use of irony, which are so much a part of the *shijo* tradition.

110 (1,392)
This poem deplores the confusion in the court in drafting a policy to deal with the Hideyoshi Invasion.

What happens if you pull down
beams and supports?
A host of opinions greet the leaning, skeleton house.
Carpenters
with rulers and ink keep milling around.

111 (331)

A political allegory on the fate of prominent men who fall from grace.

> The tree is diseased;
> no one rests in its pavilion.
> When it stood tall and verdant, no one passed it by.
> But the leaves
> have fallen, the boughs are broken; not even birds perch there now.

112 (1,858)

> Why does that pine tree stand
> so near the road?
> I wish it stood a little back, perhaps in the hollow behind.
> Everyone
> geared with rope and axe will want to cut it down.

113 (93)

> White gull,
> floating on the water,
> it was an accident my spit hit you on the back.
> White gull,
> don't be angry: I spat because the world is a dirty place.

114 (1,223)

> A sudden shower
> splatters the lotus leaf,
> but I cannot find the track of water.
> I wish my heart
> were like that leaf, that nothing ever stained it.

115 (431)

> Shall I put my worries aside
> and sigh after another's smiles?
> Shall I put my cup aside and join another club?
> What can change
> the pristine jade-like quality of my heart?

116 (2,232)

Where is that boat going,
buffeted by stormy seas?
Black clouds are bundled in the sky; why did it sail?
Be careful,
sailors of fragile craft!

117 (1,577)

Take all the misfortunes
of our household,
drop them not on men; hang them on a tree.
In wind and wet
they'll fade naturally away.

118 (2,340)

This poem, sometimes attributed to Yu Hŭiryŏng (1480–?), is structurally unusual: the first part of the final *chang* (line 4) has only two syllables.

Butterflies hover in pairs where flower blossoms are thick;
orioles perch in pairs on the branches of green willows.
Flying creatures, crawling creatures, all are in pairs.
Tell me,
why am I alone without a mate?

119 (2,066)

Pearly raindrops on green hills,
how can you deceive me?
Sedge rain cape and horsehair hat, how can you deceive me?
Two days ago
I took off my silk robes; now nothing soilable remains.

120 (77)

I'm fifty now, no longer young:
yet wherever I go, at the mere sight of wine,
I break into a broad toothy grin. Why, why?
Wine is an old,
old acquaintance; I can never forget him.

121 (1,328)
*Paduk* (Go) is a very popular board game.

> The lad has gone to dig fernbrake;
> the bamboo grove is empty.
> Who will pick up the pieces scattered across the *paduk* board?
> Reclined
> against a pine tree root, inebriate, I do not feel the approach of day.

122 (2,281)
The *jiggy* is an A-frame, a wooden carrying frame strapped to the bearer's back.

> Let's drink a cup of wine; let's drink another!
> With petals from flowers we've cut, let's mark our cups; let's drink and
> drink, let's drink forever!
> For when at last this body dies, it will be wrapped in a straw mat and
> strapped to a *jiggy*, or, perhaps, it will be borne on an elegantly decked
> bier, ten thousand standard bearers shedding tears. Either way, once
> among the reeds and rushes, the oaks and willows, when the sun is
> yellow and the moon is white, when fine rain falls or thick snowflakes
> flurry, when whirlwinds blow a mournful dirge, who will offer me
> a cup?
> Need I add:
> when monkeys whistle on my grave, won't it be too late for regrets?

123 (2,261)

> Husband and wife
> are one body in two,
> meant to grow old together, to go in death together.
> Why, then,
> does that doting old fool glare at me so?

124 (711)
The *kat* is the traditional Korean horsehair hat; the cowl is the monk's cowl.

> Village people,
> let's do what is right.
> A man born into this world who doesn't do what is right
> is like
> a horse or a cow being fed with a *kat* and cowl on its head?

125 (89)

> People of Kangwŏn Province,
> do not bring your brothers to trial.
> Servants and fields are easily acquired,
> but where
> can a brother find a brother? Don't glower at each other so.

126 (1,675)

> Listen, my good man,
> how can you live like this:
> cooking pots broken, gourds all gone?
> Need I add:
> When all you have is wheat bran and rice chaff, to whom will you look
>     for support?

127 (1,485)

> It's full daylight now;
> let's take our hoes and go.
> When I finish my fields, I'll help you weed yours.
> On the way back
> we'll pick mulberry leaves and feed the silkworms.

128 (1,221)

Chŏng Ch'ŏl was noted for his devotion to the king. Loyalty poems were often couched in the language of a lover to his beloved.

> Snow falling in the pine forest,
> every branch a flower.
> I'll cut a branch and send it to my love.
> If my love
> but see it first, what matter though it melt?

129 (419)

> I'll cut out my heart
> to form a moon
> and hang brightly in a far corner of the sky.
> Then I'll go
> to my love and shine my light upon him.

130 (1,670)

Were I brilliant,
my love would not forsake me.
Better be ordinary, for then I could stroll with my love.
Not even
being ordinary, I fear I'll never see my love.

131 (317)

Two stone Buddhas, naked and fasting,
face each other on the road.
Exposed to wind, rain, snow, and frost they may be,
but of human
parting they know nothing! For this I envy them.

132 (811)

A shadow is reflected in the water:
a monk is crossing the bridge.
Monk, stay a moment; let me ask you where you're going.
Stick pointed
at white clouds, he passes without a backward glance.

133 (1,588)

Somehow or other
my time has almost gone.
Bustling, shoving; what have I achieved?
So be it:
people keep saying, "Enough, enough!" What can I do but enjoy myself?

134 (383)

Somewhere on Namsan Mountain
Scrivener Ko has built his straw hut.
He has given it flowers and a moon, rocks and water.
Even wine
he has provided, and he's asked me to visit.

135 (1,811)

Yesterday I heard that Master Sŏng
from over the hill has new wine.
I kicked the ox to its feet, threw on a saddlecloth, and rode up here.

Boy,
is your master home? Tell him Chŏng Ch'ŏl has come.

### 136 (113)

As I move the goosefoot forward
the great string of the *kŏmun'go* resounds,
like water once ice-bound bursting now from its stream.
Somewhere
rain falls on lotus leaves; is it trying to match the sound?

### 137 (337)

When did the leaves come out,
already they're falling in the autumn breeze.
The ice and snow have melted, spurring spring flowers into bloom.
No news yet
from my love. I am greatly saddened.

### 138 (1,481)

If I lifted my wings
and flapped them twice or thrice,
I'd see my beloved on the highest peak of Pongnaesan.
But what's the point
in discussing things that are impossible?

### 139 (313)

Whether I eat wheat bran or rice chaff,
whether I have a gourd dipper or not,
in a world that is in total disarray,
if my lovely love
will but love me, faith will sustain my life.

### 140 (1,776)

Sleep-bound birds fly home;
the new moon rises.
"Monk," I cry, to the lone figure crossing the single-log bridge:
"How far to
your temple? I can hear the beating of the drum."

141 (1,264)

> Stock from boiled bitter greens
> is tastier than meat.
> My straw hut is tiny, but it best suits my station.
> My problem is
> this longing for my love: it fills my heart with care.

142 (1,531)

The poem is built around a pun on a *kisaeng's* name.

> Genuine jade, they said;
> I thought it mere imitation.
> Now that I see it, I must admit, it is indeed pure jade.
> I have
> a fleshy awl and with it I will drill.

143 (1,911)

> After a ten-year interval I see again
> the white jade wine cup in the Royal Academy.
> The clear white sheen is as it was yesterday.
> But the heart
> of a man, why does it change morning and evening?

144 (2,370)

Taebang Fortress is present-day Namwŏn in North Chŏlla Province.

> The rise and fall of nations are myriad;
> Taebang Fortress is covered with autumn grass.
> To the herdsman's pipes I'll leave my ignorance of the past
> and I'll drink
> a cup to this great age of peace.

145 (1,272)

> We'll strain sour wine and drink
> till we can't abide the taste.
> We'll boil bitter greens and chew till they become sweet.
> We'll stay
> on the road till the nails that hold the heels to our clogs are worn away.

146 (1,295)

A Shilla pagoda, eight hundred years old,
rises high in the sky.
The heavy metal drum it houses grows increasingly resonant with each
    successive beat,
highlighting
the twilight view across the field of a solitary mountain pavilion.

147 (2,081)

Crane, flying high
above the clouds in the blue sky,
do you come among us because man is so good?
That crane
will not leave though its long feathers all fall out.

148 (2,106)

Qu Yuan (340–278 B.C.) was banished as a result of palace intrigue in an-
cient China. He died by drowning. The reference here is to his loyal heart.

Fishermen of the Cho River,
do not fish these waters.
Qu Yuan's bitterness is in the bellies of the fish.
You can boil
the fish, but you can't boil out the loyalty of Qu Yuan's heart.

149 (2,313)

Big brother, little brother,
touch each other's flesh.
Who gave you birth? You are so alike.
Suckled at
the same breast, don't harbor divided hearts.

150 (266)

When our droopy-eared horse
goes for a load of salt,
anyone can tell he's good for a thousand *li*.
Why is it
the men of today think of him only as fat?

151 (51)

A man turns aside from the road
a woman walks;
and a woman turns aside from the road a man walks.
So ask not
the name of one who is neither husband nor wife.

152 (104)

I promised to return to rivers and lakes,
but I've had ten busy years.
The white gulls, unaware of the facts, chide me for being late,
but the king's
favor is so precious, I must repay it before I go back.

153 (751)

When the paulownia leaves fell
I knew it was autumn.
A fine drizzle falls on the blue river: the night air is chilly.
I left my love
a thousand *li* away; I cannot sleep tonight.

154 (762)

Forty thousand boxes of bright jewels
caught in the lotus leaves.
Gathered, measured, where shall I send them?
Pattering drops,
they are so vibrantly gay!

155 (1,101)

Now that I'm keeper of the state guesthouse
visitors throng this way.
Bows when they come; bows when they go; bows, bows, bows by
    the score.
One careful
look reveals it's all a dreadful bore.

156 (1,102)

> Now that I'm keeper of the state guesthouse
> I don my sedge cape and rain hat.
> A gentle breeze angles the fine rain. I slant a fishing pole across
>    my shoulder,
> the first of
> many trips to a river bank of red knotweed and white water-chestnut.

157 (1,103)

> Now that I'm keeper of the state guesthouse
> I close the brushwood gate again.
> I throw myself among flowing waters and blue mountains; these I take
>    as friends.
> Boy,
> should a caller say he's from Pyŏkche, tell him I'm out.

158 (402)

> Husband dead;
> tears flow down my breasts.
> Milk salted; the infant frets.
> What sort of man
> would ask me to be his?

## Sŏ Ik (1542–87)

Sŏ Ik was governor of Ŭiju. On one occasion when Yi Yulgok was the victim of a slanderous attack, Sŏ Ik wrote a letter to the king defending his friend. The king was incensed and immediately dismissed Sŏ Ik from his post. The poem expresses the poet's sense of rejection but also his unswerving loyalty. "North" implies the direction of the king. When the king met his retainers, he faced south and they faced north.

159 (497)

> I'm like a horse without a bridle
> on a green river bank after rain.
> From time to time I lift my head and neigh toward the north,
> for as the evening sun
> crosses the mountain, I long to see my lord.

## Han Ho (1543–1605)

Han Ho, better known as Han Sŏkbong, was born in Kaesŏng in 1543. He was a county chief, but his reputation rests in his skill as a calligrapher rather than as an administrator. Someone described his style as "an enraged lion pulling up grass and a thirsty giraffe running toward the river." One suspects that this is high praise, although the English equivalent may leave something to be desired. *Makkŏlli* is raw or unrefined rice wine.

### 160 (1,942)

Don't bring out the straw mat;
can't I sit on the fallen leaves?
Don't light a pine-knot torch; last night's moon is rising again.
Boy,
don't say there's no *makkŏlli* or mountain greens; bring them out.

## Cho Hŏn (1544–92)

Cho Hŏn was a scholar-official under Sŏnjo. During the Hideyoshi War, he raised an army, which he personally commanded. He died in a subsequent engagement. During the reign of Yŏngjo, he was posthumously promoted to the rank of prime minister.

### 161 (1,921)

Rain plashes the lotus pond;
mist shrouds the willows.
The boatman has gone; he's tied up his empty boat.
A seagull,
mate lost, flies to and fro in the evening sun.

### 162 (1,948)

I sit at the fishing hole,
my line cast in blue water.
Raindrops on crystal water sound even better in the fading light.
On a willow branch
I'll string my catch and bring it to the wineshop in Apricot Village.

## Yi Sunshin (1545–98)

Yi Sunshin was the famous Korean admiral who invented the turtle ship and defeated numerically superior Japanese forces in a series of naval battles during the Hideyoshi War. In this poem the admiral meditates on the lonely responsibilities of the commander-in-chief. The pipe is a reference to his Chinese allies. Some doubt has been cast on the authorship of the poem, but in the hearts of the Korean people it will always be associated with the redoubtable admiral.

163 (2,267)

> The moon is bright tonight. I sit alone
> in the lookout on Hansan Island,
> my great-sword slung at my side, my spirit deeply troubled.
> From somewhere
> the shrill note of a pipe cuts into my heart.

## Kim Changsaeng (1548–1631)

Kim Changsaeng, a pupil of Yi Yulgok, retired early from official life and gathered some disciples to whom he devoted himself. He was recalled to the bureaucracy, but sickness forced him to decline the position.

164 (623)

> I plant bamboo; that's my fence.
> I cultivate pine; that's my pavilion.
> Who knows I live here covered by white clouds?
> The cranes
> maundering in a corner of the yard are my friends.

## Im Che (1549–87)

Im Che was a sixteenth-century bohemian who failed to advance very high in the civil service because of his controversial style of life. He is said to have recited this poem when he visited the grave of Hwang Chini, a famous sixteenth-century *kisaeng*, on his way to take up an official appointment in P'yŏngyang.

165 (2,087)

> Are you asleep or are you just resting
> in this mountain valley thick with grass?
> Where is your rose complexion? Is only a skeleton buried here?
> Sad to say
> there's no one to offer me a cup of wine.

166 (965)

Im Che had quite a reputation for success with the ladies. He is said to have challenged a *kisaeng* named Hanu (literally "cold rain") with the following poem.

> The northern sky was clear,
> so I set out without rain gear.
> Snow fell on the mountain; cold rain ran through the fields.
> Today I met
> Cold Rain; I'll freeze in bed tonight.

## Hanu (sixteenth century)

The *kisaeng* Hanu reputedly met Im Che's challenge with a poem of her own. The mandarin duck symbolizes warm affection between spouses.

167 (1,411)

> What's all this about freezing in bed,
> why should you freeze in bed tonight?
> Where's your duck-embroidered pillow, your kingfisher quilt: why do
>     you say you'll freeze?
> Today you met
> Cold Rain; perhaps you'll melt in bed tonight.

## Sŏnjo (1552–1608)

In 1567 Sŏnjo succeeded Myŏngjong to the throne. A lover of the arts and learning, he promoted a number of scholarly men to high rank in the government, among them Yi Hwang, Yi Yulgok, and Chŏng Ch'ŏl. However, the period was dominated by internal factional fighting among the *yangban* (noble) families, and militarily the country was in a shambles when Hideyoshi invaded at the end of the century. Sŏnjo composed the following poem in 1572 when his friend No Chin resigned from court. The king sent a messenger carrying the poem on a silver tray. No Chin already had crossed the Han River on his way home.

168 (1,500)

> You're no sooner here than you want to go;
> when you go you don't return.
> Coming and going, we never seem to really meet.
> Today you say
> you're going again; sadness fills my heart.

## Cho Chonsŏng (1553–1627)

Cho Chonsŏng was an official who served in the government from the time of Myŏngjong to Injo. He fell from favor early in his career, but Sŏnjo restored him to an official position during the Hideyoshi War. During the Manchu Invasion he accompanied the crown prince to Chŏnju in his capacity as minister of taxes. He died soon after he returned to Seoul.

169 (1,331)

> Boy, get ready my rain gear and bamboo hat;
> the rain has cleared in East Valley.
> I'll tie a barbless hook on my long fishing pole.
> Fish, fear not,
> sheer pleasure is what I'm about.

## Song T'a (sixteenth century)

Song T'a was a singer in the reign of Sŏnjo: precise dates are not available.

170 (Shim 3,113)

> A night of wind and snow:
> I face a plum tree in my mountain home.
> I smile at it; it smiles at me.
> Well we might,
> for the plum is me and I am it.

## Yi Tŏkhyŏng (1561–1613)

Yi Tŏkhyŏng, an official who attained the rank of prime minister, eventually fell victim to factional fighting and retired to the country, where he died. He is so renowned for his tricks as a young boy that he still figures in children's comic books. The poem is based on Li Bai's *Ba jiu wen yue*.

171 (599)

> The moon is clear and round,
> hanging in a blue-black sky.
> Well might it have fallen in the winds and frosts of time,
> but it lights
> the merry guest's golden jug tonight.

## Yi Tŏg'il (1561–1622)

Yi Tŏg'il served with distinction during the Hideyoshi War, eventually attaining the rank of general. However, during the reign of Kwanghaegun he became disillusioned with the world and retired to the countryside.

172 (710)

> Stop, stop,
> stop this fight.
> Fairly, and without prejudice, stop it, stop!
> Believe me,
> if you stop this fight, a time of peace will follow.

## Kim Sang'yong (1561–1637)

Kim Sang'yong had a long career in the public service, ultimately attaining the rank of minister of justice. Entrusted with the defense of Kanghwa Island during the Manchu Invasion, he committed suicide when the island fell to the enemy. The second poem is based on *Ye zhi shi*, by the Song poet Wang Anshi (1021–86).

173 (1,013)

> Love is a lie;
> when my love says he loves me, that's a lie.
> When he says he sees me in his dreams, that's a bigger lie.
> If sleep
> eluded him as it eludes me, how could he see me in his dreams?

174 (286)

> The incense in the golden censer has all burned out;
> the drops in the water clock sound thin.
> Where have you been? To whom have you given your love?
> Moon shadows
> are on the verandah; and now you come to take my pulse!

## Pak Inno (1561–1642)

Pak Inno was born in North Kyŏngsang Province. Raised in the country, he showed unusual literary abilities from an early age. When the Hideyoshi War broke out in 1592, he was still a student. He gave up his studies, joined the army, and served with distinction throughout the entire war. In 1599 he passed the military service examination and was appointed a garrison commander on Koje Island. He held several other military appointments during his career and was invariably admired and respected by soldiers and civilians for his honesty, courage, and courtesy. After the war the old prejudice against the military establishment in the civil service reasserted itself, and Pak Inno retired to his native place, where he devoted himself to studying the Confucian classics and writing poetry. Sixty-seven *shijo* poems are extant, in addition to seven *kasa* and a number of *hanshi* (Chinese) poems. He is highly regarded as a *kasa* poet, but his *shijo* are considered too didactic and moralistic and too filled with Chinese allusions and sentiments. Some of the poems are titled, which is rather rare in shijo.

175 (1,712) Filial Piety 2 (from *The Five Cardinal Virtues*)

> In a lifespan of a hundred years
> a man becomes acquainted with all disease.
> Who knows how many years a man may serve his parents?
> Believe me:
> begin early; the duty of filial piety is never fully discharged.

176 (935) Moon Spew Peak

> The moon rising above the peak
> throws light across the mountain.
> Sky's infinity is wide and high.
> High mountain
> stuck in the sky; it's like flying over a rock.

177 (86) Hwari Terrace

> Where the towering mountain slopes down to the river,
> a huge stone stands beneath a pine.
> Surrounded by misty luminous mountain folds,
> it's as if
> the scene were freshly painted on a mica folding screen.

178 (298) Looking at Jade Bridge

> I lay down at the fishing hole.
> When I awoke the moon was bright.
> A goosefoot stick slanted in my hand, I came across Jade Bridge.
> Only sleeping birds
> know Jade Bridge's crystal sound.

179 (1,214) The Place of Medicinal Herbs
Pak Inno translates into the *shijo* form a very famous poem by the Tang poet
Jia Dao (788–843), *Xun yin zi bu yu.*

> I asked the lads beneath the pine:
> where has your master gone?
> He went to dig medicinal herbs; he should have been back by now.
> Clouds lie thick
> across the mountain; impossible to tell where he has gone.

180 (976)

> The drum beats in a distant temple;
> how distant can that temple be?
> Above the blue mountain, I know; below the white clouds, I feel sure.
> Today, too,
> white clouds shroud the world; where that temple is I do not know.

181 (1,092)

> With the new moon hanging
> above the mountain ridge,
> and sleep-bound birds flitting through the woods, I reach the single-
> log bridge.
> I don't know
> how far the temple is, but I can hear the evening bell tolling crystal clear.

182 (126) Kyŏkchin Peak

> This remote mountain peak
> towers above a troubled world.
> My deaf, deaf ears become deafer still whenever I wash them clean,
> and rights and wrongs
> beyond this mountain I cannot hear, I cannot see.

## Kang Pokchung (1563–1639)

Very little is known about Kang Pokchung other than that he was an official. His poems have only recently been discovered, and his work awaits critical evaluation. However, even a cursory examination of the sixty-four *shijo* with which he is credited reveals a considerable poetic talent.

183 (Shim 1,174)

> Having lived a modest hundred years,
> one morning I'll become an Immortal.
> Mornings astride the clouds, evenings astride the rain, ten thousand *li*
>    I'll fly, soaring through the sky.
> Only then
> shall I grow old, with heaven and earth, moon and sun.

184 (Shim 1,510)

> The moon is bright,
> but where has my old friend gone?
> When he looks at the moon, does he, too, think as I?
> Looking at the moon
> and thinking of my friend, sadness fills my heart.

185 (Shim 565)
*Kasa* was a genre of vernacular verse.

My heart is restless,
so I compose a *kasa* poem.
The righteous all say to compose is fine,
but floating clouds
that hide the sun say such composition is wrong.

186 (Shim 206)

Pick the flower, if you will,
but do not cut the branch.
If you cut the branch, where can the flower bloom?
Secure in
this knowledge, there's nothing we can harm.

187 (Shim 2,266)

The white gulls
of Yullyŏng Stream said to me:
"Grow old, we beg you, ignorant of the rights and wrongs of men.
We are called
black and white for things we never said."

## *Shin Hŭm (1566–1628)*

Shin Hŭm was a scholar-official during the reign of Sŏnjo. He was one of six prominent men asked by the dying Sŏnjo to support Prince Yŏngch'ang as heir to the throne, and this cost him his official post when Kwanghaegun became king. He returned to his home in Ch'unch'ŏn. However, he was restored to office after Injo's successful coup d'état against Kwanghaegun.

188 (473)

The song maker
is a man of many worries.
Through song he strives for the relief words have failed to bring.
Believe me:
were such relief real, I, too, would sing.

189 (1,424)

> Last night after the rain
> the pomegranates burst into bloom.
> On the bank of the lotus pond I rolled up the crystal bead curtain.
> Why can I never
> allay the fears of a deeply troubled heart?

190 (1,324)

> Rain fell in the morning;
> later the wind blew.
> Ten thousand *li* to go, why should it rain and blow?
> So be it:
> twilight is still far removed, why not rest before I go?

191 (410)

> With the blood from my wounded heart
> I'll paint a likeness of my love.
> I'll hang it on a high white wall and view it there.
> Who invented
> parting; did he mean to kill?

192 (457)

> White heron beside the stream,
> why do you stand so?
> Why spy on fish so unconcerned by your presence?
> Listen:
> you share the same water, why not forget them?

193 (528)
The poem refers to the ancient world before writing was invented when the tying of knots was a means of communication.

> I was born too late to witness
> the affairs of the ancient world.
> When the knot fell into desuetude, the affairs of men grew complex.
> Better
> drop into a wine village and forget the world.

194 (1,278)

> After leaving the world,
> honor and dishonor become irrelevant.
> After the *kŏmun'go* and a book, I feel myself at leisure.
> White gull,
> you and I have forgotten the complexities of the world.

195 (2,310)

> Crossbeams long or short,
> uprights crooked or warped;
> do not mock my grass hut for being small.
> Remember:
> the moon on the mountain vines is also mine.

196 (1,061)

> Snow falls on a mountain village;
> the rocky road is buried.
> Don't open the brushwood gate; who is there to visit me?
> The night's
> bright crescent moon is my only friend.

197 (380)

The elixir was to be found on the three mountains where the Immortals dwelt. The mulberry patch becoming the blue sea is a reference to a very changeable world.

> I plowed three furrows
> deep in a Namsan valley.
> From the mountains of the gods I dug the elixir roots and planted
>     them here.
> Alone
> I shall watch the mulberry patch blue into the sea.

## Chang Man (1566–1629)

Chang Man held a number of official posts in court during the reign of Kwanghaegun. Foreseeing the downfall of the tyrant, he retired from office and went to live in the country. During the reign of Injo, he returned to office and gave notable assistance in putting down the rebellion of Yi Kwal.

However, he was held responsible for the loss of a battle during the Manchu Invasion of 1627 and was exiled to Puyŏ. In consideration of his past noble service to the country, he was forgiven, recalled, and put in office again.

In old Korea oxen did the plowing. The stormy seas represent the factional fighting at court, and boat and horse refer to the administrative and military arms of the government, respectively. The poet reaches the sensible conclusion that he should give up public service and devote himself to farming.

198 (2,231)

> A boatman frightened by stormy seas
> sold his boat and bought a horse,
> but the twisted entrails of mountain paths were worse than any peril
>     at sea.
> From now on,
> perhaps, he'll forget his boat and horse and confine himself to plowing
>     the fields.

## Kim Tŏngnyŏng (1567–96)

Kim Tŏngnyŏng was skilled in military affairs. During the Hideyoshi War, he raised an army and was appointed general. However, in 1596 he was falsely accused of being involved in Yi Monghak's rebellion. He was arrested, tortured, and thrown into jail, where he died. He is supposed to have composed the following song while languishing in jail. The fire refers to Hideyoshi's invasion; the flowers to the young men who made the supreme sacrifice.

199 (2,149)

> The spring mountain is on fire,
> burning flowers yet to bloom.
> Water can quench that mountain fire,
> but a smokeless
> fire that water cannot quench burns on within me.

## Chŏng On (1569–1641)

Chŏng On was exiled to Cheju Island by Kwanghaegun for supporting the claims of Prince Yŏngch'ang to the throne. He remained there till Injo became king and recalled him to the court. However, the Manchu Invasion left

him with such a sense of deep personal disgrace that he retired from court to
a mountain retreat where he died in 1641.

200 (1,972)

> I close my book and open the window;
> there's a boat floating on the lake.
> What do the white gulls think about as they fly leisurely to and fro?
> Ah, to hell
> with fame, I'll go and frolic with you.

## Kim Kwang'uk (1580–1656)

Kim Kwang'uk was an official of the court during the reigns of Sŏnjo,
Kwanghaegun, and Injo. In 1615 Kwanghaegun dismissed him from office.
He returned to his hometown of Haeju, where he wrote a series of fourteen
poems called *Songs of Chestnut Village*, based on the poems of the Chinese
poet Tao Qian (Tao Yuanming; 365–427). Coincidentally, both poets lived
in a place called Chestnut Village, both had served in public life, and both
had returned to the simple joys of nature. The similarity in circumstances
prompted Kim Kwang'uk to compose his cycle of poems from which the fol-
lowing are taken.

201 (175)

> Fame I've forgotten;
> riches and high station I've forgotten.
> I've forgotten all the worries of this world.
> I've even
> forgotten myself. How could people not forget me?

202 (2,134)

> Rowing a skiff alone
> on the bright moonlit autumn river,
> I throw out a line and surprise sleeping white gulls.
> From somewhere
> the sound of a fisherman's pipe also helps the mood.

203 (620)

Bamboo stick, the sight of you
fills me with trust and delight.
Ah, boyhood days when you were my horse!
Stand there now
behind the window, and when we go out, let me stand behind you.

204 (1,187)

I cut a slender willow branch
and string on it the day's catch.
I cross a tumbledown bridge in search of a wine house.
The entire valley
is heaped with fallen apricot blossoms: I cannot find the way.

205 (1,941)

Using a clean-scrubbed pot
and spring water from beneath the rock,
I cook to sweetness red-bean rice gruel. Add to this *kimch'i* seasoned
    just with salt.
Here are two
pleasures of the palate I fear others may discover.

## Kim Yuk (1580–1658)

Kim Yuk was a scholar-official who served in a variety of positions in the
bureaucracy during the reigns of Sŏnjo and Hyojong, finally attaining the
rank of prime minister.

206 (1,761)

When the wine in your house matures
be sure to ask me over.
When my flowers bloom I'll certainly invite you.
Our topic:
how to forget the cares of a hundred years.

## Hong Ikhan (1586–1637)

Hong Ikhan was an official in the Office of the Inspector General. He was carried off by the Qing during the Manchu Invasion of 1636 for his refusal to consider peace terms. He refused to compromise, and eventually he was killed.

207 (1,682)

> The day we parted I cannot say
> whether blood tears were shed,
> but in the waters of the Amnok there was not a trace of blue,
> and the old
> white-haired boatman said he'd never seen the like before.

## Yun Sŏndo (1587–1671)

Yun Sŏndo, regarded by most Korean commentators as the greatest of the *shijo* poets, is another in the long list of poet-ministers who had turbulent political careers. He passed the civil-service examination at the *chinsa* level when he was twenty-six, but he did not serve under the tyrant Kwanghaegun. In 1616, he presented a memorial to the king remonstrating against corruption in the court, for which he was duly exiled to Kyŏnwŏn, where he spent the next thirteen years and is said to have written his earliest poems. He was recalled in 1623 when Injo succeeded to the throne. In 1628 he was appointed personal tutor to the two young princes, Pongnim and Inp'yŏng. He got into trouble again during the Manchu Invasion of 1636 for failing to attend on the king. He was sent in exile to Yŏngdŏk but was soon released. Over the next number of years he wrote a series of memorials to the king, which kept getting him into trouble. The final embroilment occurred over the length of the mourning period that was adjudged appropriate for Hyojong's mother. Again Yun Sŏndo's opponents carried the day, and the poet was banished to Samsu, where he remained until his release in 1668. Seventy-six of his *shijo* poems are extant.

The following, including "Song Of Five Friends," are from *New Songs in the Mountains*. They reveal the poet's joy in nature and show his determination to leave the confusion of political life and retire to the simple life of the hermit. The poems are titled, which is rather rare in *shijo*.

208 (1,045) Natural Joy 1

I'm building a straw hut beneath a rock
in a landscape of mountain and water.
Those who do not understand laugh at what they see,
but folly
and rustic simplicity somehow seem to become me.

209 (924) Natural Joy 2

After eating my fill
of barley and young greens,
I relax to my heart's content by the stream beneath the rocks.
Other things
in life, why covet them?

210 (1,772) Natural Joy 3

Wine cup in hand, I sit alone
looking at those distant mountains.
Were my love coming, would my joy be quite so great?
The mountains
neither speak nor laugh; yet they are always good.

211 (429) Natural Joy 5

Lazy I am:
Heaven knows this well.
Of all the many affairs of men not one has it entrusted to me.
Mine it is
to watch over rivers and mountains, for this demands no rival struggle.

212 (1,943) At the Beginning of the Banquet 1

How is a house built?
It is the work of a master carpenter.
Why are the timbers straight? They follow the line of ink and ruler.
Knowledge
of this home truth will bring you long life.

213 (1,253) At the Beginning of the Banquet 2

> How do you make good wine?
> It's in the mixing of the yeast.
> How do you make good soup? It's in the adding of the condiments.
> Knowledge
> of this culinary truth will bring you long life.

214 (1,239) Song at the End of the Banquet 2

> Wine without virtue
> leads to violence.
> Dancing without decorum leads to vulgarity.
> Believe me:
> the man of virtue and decorum lives ten thousand years.

215 (1,452) Singing of First Light in Spring

> Have the rigors of winter passed?
> where have the snow winds gone?
> Spring's breath shimmers across a thousand, ten thousand hills.
> I'll open
> the lattice door at daybreak and look at the light in the sky.

216 (986) Song of Summer Rain 1

> It's raining; we can't go to the fields.
> Shut the brushwood gate; feed the ox.
> Summer rain is always like this; see to the plow and implements.
> Rest now,
> and when you see the weather clear, plow the long-furrowed field.

217 (827) Song of Deep Night

> The wind is up; close the lattice door.
> It's late; put out the light.
> I'll lie down, with my head on the pillow, and rest as long as I can.
> Boy,
> when it brightens in the morning, rouse me from my sleep.

218 (1,129) Song of the Setting Sun

> After the sun goes down
> the mountain air is fine,

but with the approach of twilight, the landscape darkens.
Boy,
tigers are scary: don't go wandering around.

219 (1,960) Autumn Night Tune
In this allegory the blowflies refer to small-minded men, and the beautiful
refers to the king.

The blowflies are gone;
I lay down my flyswatter.
Leaves fall; the beautiful grow old.
Moonlight shines
brightly in the bamboo grove: this I joy to see.

220 (840) Singing an Old Melody

I string my old, neglected *kayagŭm*,
and begin to play.
A graceful melody from the past provides a happy sound.
No one
could possibly know my song; I return the instrument to its case.

221 (1,266) Song of Consolation in Banishment 1
This poem was written after the poet was banished to Kyŏngwŏn by
Kwanghaegun.

Sad or glad,
right or wrong,
all I have to do is hone and hone the heart.
Why concern
myself with all those other things?

222 (423) 1. Song of Five Friends

You ask how many friends I have?
Water, rocks, pine, and bamboo.
And when the moon rises over east mountain, I feel even
    greater pleasure.
Enough:
to these five why add more?

223 (222) 2

> How clean the color of the clouds,
> yet they often turn black.
> How clear the sound of the wind, yet it often stops blowing.
> Water only
> is truly clean and constant.

224 (157) 3

> Why do flowers fall
> so quickly after they blossom?
> Why does grass turn yellow when it has just greened?
> It seems
> as if only rocks are impervious to change.

225 (646) 4

"Nine Springs" means deep in the earth or the afterworld.

> Flowers bloom when it's hot;
> leaves fall when it's cold.
> Pine, you are impervious to snow and frost?
> Thus I know
> your roots reach straight to the Nine Springs.

226 (332) 5

> Neither wood,
> nor grass;
> who made it straight, why is it hollow?
> So green
> all the year round; that's why I like it.

227 (1,816) 6

> Tiny object floating high,
> lighting all the world,
> is any other light as bright throughout the night sky?
> You see everything
> but say nothing; you are, indeed, my friend.

## The Fisherman's Calendar

*The Fisherman's Calendar* is a cycle of forty poems describing the four seasons in one of Yun Sŏndo's favorite retreats. The fisherman is a time-honored symbol of the wise man who lives simply in nature. There is a solid tradition of poems treating this theme both in China and Korea.

Yun Sŏndo was inspired to write his poem when reworking the earlier "Fisherman's Song" by Yi Hyŏnbo (in which Yi T'oegye collaborated), which in turn was a reworking into nine verses of an anonymous poem from Koryŏ.

*The Fisherman's Calendar* shows some differences in syllable count from the regular *shijo* pattern. In addition, it features two refrains that are not found in *shijo*. The first refrain varies in a regular pattern through the verses; it describes various tasks on the boat, pushing off, raising sail, lowering sail, rowing, and the like. The second refrain is onomatopoeic: *chighukch'ong, chigukch'ong*, representing the winding of the anchor chain, and *ŏsawa*, the rhythm of the oars.

*Spring*

228 (1,352) 1

> Mist lifts on the stream in front,
> sunlight illumines the mountain behind.
>> Push away, push away!
> The night tide is almost out; soon the morning tide will be coming in.
>> *Chigukch'ong, chigukch'ong, ŏsawa!*
> Flowers
> in profusion adorn the river village; distant hues are best.

229 (369) 2

> The day is hot;
> fish jump in the water.
>> Weigh anchor, weigh anchor!
> Seagulls in twos and threes fly back and forth.
>> *Chigukch'ong, chigukch'ong, ŏsawa!*
> My fishing pole
> is ready; did I put the *makkŏlli* jar on board?

230 (679) 3

> An east wind springs up;
> waves get up a lovely swell.
>> Hoist the sail, hoist the sail!
> I leave East Lake behind, move on through to West Lake.
>> *Chigukch'ong, chigukch'ong, ŏsawa!*
> The mountain
> in front passes by, giving way to the mountain behind.

231 (1,571) 4

> Is that the cuckoo singing?
> Is that the willow grove greening?
>> Row the boat, row the boat!
> A few fisher houses glimmer in and out of the haze.
>> *Chigukch'ong, chigukch'ong, ŏsawa!*
> Shoaling fish
> flash in a clear deep pool.

232 (144) 5

The reference in the following is to the song that concludes *The Fisherman*, ascribed to the Chinese poet Qu Yuan.

> Gentle sunlight bathes the water;
> the waves are like oil.
>> Row the boat, row the boat!
> Should I cast the net; my fishing pole might be better?
>> *Chigukch'ong, chigukch'ong, ŏsawa!*
> The song of the fisherman
> stirs my heart; I forget all about the fish.

233 (1,136) 6

The offices referred to here are those of the prime minister, minister of the right, and minister of the left.

> The evening sun slants in the sky;
> enough, it's time to go home.
>> Lower the sail, lower the sail!
> Willows and flowers are new at every bend.
>> *Chigukch'ong, chigukch'ong, ŏsawa!*

Shall I look
with envy on the three highest offices in the land or think of the affairs
     of men?

### 234 (866) 7

There are echoes here of a famous Chinese poem, *Chuan zi he shang shi,* describing a fisherman who has no luck fishing but settles for a boatload of moonlight: "The night is quiet, the water cold, / the fish will not bite. / I load my empty boat with moonlight / and come on home" (see no. 40, p. 46).

> I long to walk on fragrant grasses,
> to pick orchids and gromwells, too.
>      Heave to, heave to!
> What have I loaded in my tiny leaf-like boat?
>      *Chigukch'ong, chigukch'ong, ōsawa!*
> On the way out,
> I was alone; on the way back, I have the moon.

### 235 (2,169) 8

The Peach Paradise refers to the utopia discovered by the fisherman in the "Preface to the Peach Blossom Spring" by Tao Qian (Tao Yuanming, 365–427). The fisherman announces his discovery on his return to the world, but he is unable to find the Peach Paradise again.

> Tipsy, I stretch out;
> what if I drift through the fast water?
>      Tie up, tie up!
> Petals drift by in the water; the Peach Paradise must be near.
>      *Chigukch'ong, chigukch'ong, ōsawa!*
> How well hidden
> from the red dust of the world of men!

### 236 (348) 9

> I hang up my fishing line,
> look at the moon through the rush-awning window.
>      Drop anchor, drop anchor!
> Has night fallen already? The cuckoo's call is limpid on the air.
>      *Chigukch'ong, chigukch'ong, ōsawa!*
> Excitement
> unabated, I forget where I'm going.

237 (439) 10

Will there be no tomorrow;
how long till the spring night sets?
Beach the boat, beach the boat!
My fishing pole is my walking stick as I head for the brushwood gate.
*Chigukch'ong, chigukch'ong, ŏsawa!*
Days like this
are a fisherman's life.

*Summer*

238 (233) 1

Protracted rain comes to an end;
the stream begins to clear.
Push away, push away!
I put my fishing pole on my shoulder; excitement grips me deep.
*Chigukch'ong, chigukch'ong, ŏsawa!*
Who painted
these layered mountain peaks in the mist-tinted river?

239 (1,469) 2

Wrap my rice in lotus leaves;
don't bother preparing side dishes.
Weigh anchor, weigh anchor!
I have my bamboo rain hat on; what did I do with my sedge rain cape?
*Chigukch'ong, chigukch'ong, ŏsawa!*
White gull,
so very impassive, are you following me or am I following you?

240 (709) 3

Wind rises in the pondweed;
it's cool at the rush-awning window.
Hoist the sail, hoist the sail!
Are summer winds steady? Let the boat drift where it will.
*Chigukch'ong, chigukch'ong, ŏsawa!*
North bank,
south river; it's all the same to me.

241 (814) 4

The reference in the first section is to the song that concludes *The Fisherman*, ascribed to Qu Yuan: "When the Canglang's waters are clear, / I can wash my hat strings in them; / when the Canglang's waters are muddy, / I can wash my feet in them." The admonition is to seek official preferment when times are good, and to retire gracefully when times are bad. The middle section refers to Fu Cha of Wu who was so angry at the suicide of his servant Wu Yuan that he had the body put in a sack and thrown into the Wu River. The final section refers to Qu Yuan again. A minister in the kingdom of Chu, he was banished for objecting to official policy. Distressed, he committed suicide. The idea here is that the poet might catch Qu Yuan's soul in a fish. Overall, the poem is a meditation on traditional *hyo*, or loyalty.

> So what if I wash my feet
> in muddy water?
>> Row the boat, row the boat!
> I would go to the river Wu; how sad the stormy waves of a thousand years.
>> *Chigukch'ong, chigukch'ong, ŏsawa!*
> I would go
> to the river Chu, but I might catch a fish with a human soul.

242 (724) 5

The inference here is that one should give the best fishing place to an old man just as the people of Lei gave Emperor Shun the best place in ancient times.

> In the thick shade of the willow grove,
> a mossy spot catches my eye.
>> Row the boat, row the boat!
> When I reach the bridge, I'll assign no blame in the fishermen's wrangling.
>> *Chigukch'ong, chigukch'ong, ŏsawa!*
> If I meet
> the crane-haired old man, I'll follow the example of Lei Lake.

243 (316) 6

> Excitement grips me deep;
> I had no idea day was fading fast.
>> Lower the sail, lower the sail!
> Beating time on the mast, I sing boat songs.
>> *Chigukch'ong, chigukch'ong, ŏsawa!*
> Who knows
> the old world graces embedded in these songs.

244 (1,135) 7

The first section appears to be a loose translation of a poem by the Tang poet Li Shangyin (812–58).

> The evening sun is grand,
> but twilight is close at hand.
>> Heave to, heave to!
> The path that winds across the cliff slopes down beneath the pines.
>> *Chigukch'ong, chigukch'ong, ŏsawa!*
> The song of the oriole
> studs the green grove.

245 (771) 8

The mosquitoes are small-minded men who seek only personal gain; the blowflies are even more despicable types who ruin a man by slander. The final comment would seem to be tongue in cheek as the poet battles with the various insects that trouble him. Sang Hongyang of Han was a wily economics expert who made a large personal fortune while working for his country.

> I'll spread my nets on the sand,
> lie down under the rush-awning and rest.
>> Tie up, tie up!
> The mosquitoes are a pest; are the blowflies any better?
>> *Chigukch'ong, chigukch'ong, ŏsawa!*
> My only fear
> is that the wily rogue of Han, Sang Hongyang, may be listening in.

246 (860) 9

The middle section quotes a phrase from the Tang poet Wei Yingwu (737–ca. 792): *crossing-fields-crosswise-boat.* However, the sense of the phrase seems to be a boat tied to the ferry landing strangely defying the current by sitting crosswise in the water. The final section also incorporates a phrase from the same Wei Yingwu poem: *river-edge-hidden-plant/grass.*

> Who can tell how wind and waves will change
> in the course of the night?
> > Drop anchor, drop anchor!
> Who was it said "The boat tied at the ferry cuts across the current"?
> > *Chigukch'ong, chigukch'ong, ŏsawa!*
> The hidden
> plants by the river's edge are truly lovely.

247 (1,544) 10

> I look up at my snail-shell hut;
> white clouds are all around.
> > Beach the boat, beach the boat!
> I climb the stony path, bulrush fan sideways in my hand.
> > *Chigukch'ong, chigukch'ong, ŏsawa!*
> You ask
> if a fisherman's life is leisurely; well, this is what I do.

*Autumn*

248 (799) 1

> How unspoiled the life of the fisherman,
> away from the outside world!
> > Push away, push away!
> Laugh not at an old fisherman; he's part of every painting.
> > *Chigukch'ong, chigukch'ong, ŏsawa!*
> Seasonal pleasures
> are all fine; but the autumn river is best of all.

249 (1,226) 2

> Autumn comes to the river village;
> the fish grow fat.
> > Weigh anchor, weigh anchor!
> Leisurely hours spent on broad waters.
> > *Chigukch'ong, chigukch'ong, ŏsawa!*
> I look back
> on the world of men: the farther off the better.

250 (894) 3

>White clouds get up;
>tree branches rustle.
>>Hoist the sail, hoist the sail!
>Off to West Lake on the full tide, on the ebb tide to East Lake.
>>*Chigukch'ong, chigukch'ong, ŏsawa!*
>Redshank
>blooms in the pondweed: it's a joy to see it everywhere.

251 (299) 4

>Out there where the wild geese fly
>I see peaks I've never seen before.
>>Row the boat, row the boat!
>I fish a bit, but it's the mood that really intoxicates.
>>*Chigukch'ong, chigukch'ong, ŏsawa!*
>The evening sun,
>dazzlingly bright, gold broiders a thousand peaks.

252 (1,626) 5

>How many fine silver-jade fish
>have I caught?
>>Row the boat, row the boat!
>I'll make a reed fire, select the best for broiling;
>>*Chigukch'ong, chigukch'ong, ŏsawa!*
>tilt the crock jar
>and fill the gourd dipper full.

253 (469) 6

>Wind blowing gently athwart,
>the billowing sail brings me back.
>>Lower the sail, lower the sail!
>Darkness deepens in the sky; pure pleasure remains.
>>*Chigukch'ong, chigukch'ong, ŏsawa!*
>I never tire of
>red-tinted trees and clear water.

254 (2,375) 7
The image in the first section is presumably taken from Su Shi's (Su Dongpo, 1037–1101) "Red Cliff," which describes moonlight settling on the river like dewdrops. The Phoenix Pavilion is a reference to the royal palace where the poet would wish to send the pure moonlight. Legend tells of the white hare that grinds medicinal powders on the moon.

> White dewdrops angle over the river;
> the bright moon has risen.
>> Heave to, heave to!
> Phoenix Pavilion is far away; to whom shall I give this pure light?
>> *Chigukch'ong, chigukch'ong, ŏsawa!*
> To a noble guest
> I'll feed the medicine the jade rabbit grinds.

255 (119) 8
Xu You washed his ears in the river when the emperor suggested giving him the throne. "West wind dust" is a reference to the "dust" of the outside world.

> Are heaven and earth different?
> What place is this now?
>> Tie up, tie up!
> West wind dust doesn't reach this far; no need to fan it away.
>> *Chigukch'ong, chigukch'ong, ŏsawa!*
> I've heard
> nothing; no need to wash my ears.

256 (1,541) 9

> Frost falls on my clothes;
> I do not feel cold.
>> Drop anchor, drop anchor!
> My fishing boat is cramped; is the fleeting world any bigger?
>> *Chigukch'ong, chigukch'ong, ŏsawa!*
> Tomorrow
> will be like this, as will the day after.

257 (1,218) 10

I'll go to my stone hut among the pines
and watch the moon at dawn.
    Beach the boat, beach the boat!
But how can I find the leaf-strewn path through these deserted hills?
    *Chigukch'ong, chigukch'ong, ŏsawa!*
White clouds
follow me; my hermit clothes weigh me down.

*Winter*

258 (221) 1

Winter sunlight falls thick
after the clouds have cleared.
    Push away, push away!
Ice binds heaven and earth, yet the sea remains unchanged;
    *Chigukch'ong, chigukch'ong, ŏsawa!*
billow after billow,
rolls of silk unfurled.

259 (1,887) 2
"Nets freeze" is from Du Fu.

Are line and pole in proper order;
has the boat been sealed with bamboo?
    Weigh anchor, weigh anchor!
They say nets freeze on Xiao Lake and the Xiang River.
    *Chigukch'ong, chigukch'ong, ŏsawa!*
There's no better place
for fishing now.

260 (1,464) 3

The fish have left the shallows,
gone to deeper pools.
    Hoist the sail, hoist the sail!
Let's head for the fishing grounds while the weather holds fine.
    *Chigukch'ong, chigukch'ong, ŏsawa!*
Fat fish bite,
they say, when the bait is right.

261 (59) 4

When the snow cleared last night
the whole world had changed.
     Row the boat, row the boat!
A sea of glass in front, jade mountain folds behind.
     *Chigukch'ong, chigukch'ong, ŏsawa!*
Is this where the Immortals live,
where the Buddha lives? It cannot be the world of men.

262 (277) 5

Oblivious of net and pole
I tap the lip of the boat.
     Row the boat, row the boat!
How often have I pondered going back across the river?
     *Chigukch'ong, chigukch'ong, ŏsawa!*
Those unpredictable
strong gusts, will they blow or not?

263 (1,766) 6
Li Su of the Tang released flocks of ducks and geese to conceal the movement of his troops, thus gaining victory in a battle with Wu Yuanji. The "shame of the trees" refers to the fears of the retreating troops of Fu Jian after a shattering defeat in 383: they were afraid that the enemy was concealed behind every tree.

Crows fly off to roost;
quite a few have passed me by?
     Lower the sail, lower the sail!
The road ahead darkens; snow falls in the fading light.
     *Chigukch'ong, chigukch'ong, ŏsawa!*
Who will attack
Oya Lake, and wash away the shame of the trees?

264 (583) 7

"Big-mouthed fine-scaled fish" is from the second of Su Shi's "Red Cliff" prose-poems.

> Red cliffs and green rock faces
> surround me like a painted screen.
>> Heave to, heave to!
> What matter whether or not I've caught big-mouthed fine-scaled fish?
>> *Chigukch'ong, chigukch'ong, ŏsawa!*
> I sit in my sedge cape and hat,
> heart quickening in my solitary boat.

265 (813) 8

The idea of the clouds that block out the world presumably comes from a *hanshi* poem by Ch'oe Ch'iwŏn.

> How valiant that solitary pine
> standing on the bank!
>> Tie up, tie up!
> Do not find fault with murky clouds; they block out the world.
>> *Chigukch'ong, chigukch'ong, ŏsawa!*
> Do not tire of
> roaring waves; they blot out the dust and clamor.

266 (1,969) 9

Yan Ziling retired from the court of Emperor Guangwu (r. A.D. 25–57), founder of the Latter Han dynasty; dressed in sheepskins, he spent his life fishing the Qili River. Jiang Taigong fled from the tyranny of the Shang king Zhou (ca. 11th c. B.C.) and spent ten years fishing. King Wen discovered Taigong on the banks of the Wei and brought him back as chief counselor.

> It's been said from of old
> that the sage lives in seclusion.
>> Drop anchor, drop anchor!
> Who was it that wore the sheepskin and fished the Qili River?
>> *Chigukch'ong, chigukch'ong, ŏsawa!*
> What of the man
> who fished for ten years, counting the time on his fingers?

267 (1,398) 10

> Ah! the day comes to a close
> it's time to eat and rest.
>> Beach the boat, beach the boat!
> Red petals tint the snow-filmed road as I walk merrily home.
>> *Chigukch'ong, chigukch'ong, ŏsawa!*
> Till the snow moon
> crosses West Peak, I'll keep my pine window aslant.

# PART III

## Chosŏn Dynasty: After the Hideyoshi War (1592–1910)

# Chosŏn Dynasty: After the Hideyoshi War (1592–1910)

## Yi Myŏnghan (1595–1645)

Yi Myŏnghan was a scholar-official who began his career under Kwang-haegun and served with distinction during the Manchu Invasion. He got into trouble for sending a secret message to Ming China. The representatives of the rival Qing group had him imprisoned for a time, but he was soon released. He was well versed in poetry and neo-Confucian metaphysics (sŏngnihak).

268 (254)

> If the road I walk in my dreams
> left tracks,
> I'd wear out the stone path that leads to my true love's window.
> How sad
> to have to say: alas! dreams leave no tracks.

269 (1,119)

> The sun sets behind west mountain;
> no clear edge divides earth and sky.
> Moonlight is white on white pear blossoms; thoughts of my love
>     arise anew.
> Cuckoo bird,
> what love fills your heart that you cry so through the night?

## Chŏng Tugyŏng (1597–1673)

Chŏng Tugyŏng was an official during the reign of Injo. He retired early from public life and devoted himself to scholarly pursuits. His poems were once compared to those of Li Bai and Du Fu.

270 (292)

> Of wine in brimming golden jugs
> we've drunk our fill.
> Well drunk, there's no end to our pleasure in songs that go on and on.
> Let's not talk
> about the setting sun; the moon is following fast.

## Hong Nang (sixteenth century)

Hong Nang was a celebrated *kisaeng* from Kyŏngsŏng who had a love affair with the governor of Hamgyŏng Province, Ch'oe Kyŏngch'ang. When Ch'oe was recalled to Seoul, the lovers had a tearful farewell in Yŏnghŭng. Hong Nang wrote the poem on her lonely way back to Kyŏngsŏng and sent it, along with a willow branch, a traditional symbol of parting, to her lover. Afterwards Ch'oe translated the poem into Chinese.

271 (774)

> I've cut a mountain willow, my love,
> and I'm sending it to you.
> Plant it outside your bedroom window; watch it as it grows.
> In night rain
> when new leaves sprout, think of them as me.

## Chŏng T'aehwa (1602–73)

Chŏng T'aehwa was a court official at the time of the Manchu Invasion in 1636. In the following year, he accompanied Prince Sohyŏn when the latter was taken as a hostage to the Qing court.

272 (1,257)

> Drink till merry,
> then sit in a circle.

A myriad cares announce their departure.
Boy,
fill the cup; let's speed our cares upon their way.

## Yi Yŏng (1615–37)

Yi Yŏng is known in the anthologies as Tongsan Yi Sŏnsaeng. He was killed
with his family in a battle during the Manchu Invasion.

273 (2,117)

Who sliced the crescent moon so small;
who drew the full moon so round?
Streams flow but do not dry up; smoke disappears as soon as it rises.
I don't understand
the waxing and waning of this world.

## Hyojong (1619–59)

The second son of Injo, Hyojong succeeded to the throne in 1649. Filled
with bitter memories of being held hostage in Beijing after the Manchu In-
vasion in 1636, he planned to erase the disgrace by conquering the territory
immediately north of the Korean border, but he died before he could effect
his resolve. He is said to have written this poem on his way to Beijing. The
poem seems to be political allegory, the point being that one day the posi-
tions of captive and captor might well be reversed.

274 (2,038)

Mountain flowers and grasses,
what's so amusing about the sound
of rain falling in a clear stream that you sway in mirth and laughter?
Wait and see:
spring's days are numbered; laugh while you may.

## Prince Inp'yŏng (1622–58)

Prince Inp'yŏng, the third son of Injo and younger brother of Hyojong, was
well known for his skills in political negotiation at the Qing court in China.
He was also noted for his skill in Chinese calligraphy. The poem below is

almost identical with one sung by General Ch'oe Yŏng (no. 7, p. 29), who was defeated by Yi Sŏnggye in a battle that proved decisive in the founding of the Chosŏn dynasty.

275 (833)

> Don't mock a gnarled pine
> that it has bent in the wind.
> Do spring flowers stay beautiful forever?
> In howling gale
> and driving snow, it's you who'll envy me.

## Nam Kuman (1629–1711)

Nam Kuman was a public official who had the reputation of always considering the public good ahead of personal interest. In 1678 he got embroiled in factional fighting and was exiled. However, he was brought back from exile after the Namin (Southerner) faction was defeated in 1680. Subsequently he had a distinguished career.

276 (677)

> Does dawn light the east window?
> Listen, the lark is singing.
> Has the cowherd not risen yet?
> When will he plow
> the long-furrowed field across the hill?

## Prince Nang'wŏn (?–1699)

Prince Nang'wŏn was the grandson of Sŏnjo. He was reputedly skilled in poetry and scholarly affairs. Liu Ling and Li Bai were noted for their love of wine.

277 (598) Drinking Alone Beneath the Moon

> When did the moon come up?
> Who made the wine?
> Liu Ling has gone; so, too, has Li Bai.
> With nowhere
> left to ask, I'll get drunk and enjoy myself on my own.

## Prince Yuch'ŏn (seventeenth century)

Prince Yuch'ŏn, a descendant of Sŏnjo, was noted both as a painter and a calligrapher.

278 (2,139)

Autumn mountains autumn tinted
all immersed in the autumn river.
The autumn moon rises round in the autumn sky.
In autumn frost,
a brace of wild geese wing their way south.

## Pak T'aebo (1654–89)

Pak T'aebo was an official under both Hyojong and Sukjong. In the fifteenth year of the reign of Sukjong, he was sentenced to exile on Chindo Island for writing a memorial opposing the abdication of Queen Inhyŏn. He died in Noryangjin, on his way to exile. Shen Nong was a legendary emperor in China who was noted for his skills in agriculture and medicine.

279 (2,366)

A fire blazes in my heart;
it burns my innards up.
I saw Shen Nong in a dream and asked him for a cure.
He said:
that fire springs from loyalty and indignation; nothing will put it out.

## Kim Ch'ang'ŏp (1658–1721)

Kim Ch'ang'ŏp had no interest in fame or high station. Early in life he decided to build a house in the country and devote himself to the simple delights of farming. In 1713 he accompanied his brother, Ch'angjin, when the latter went on a diplomatic mission to China. He also accompanied his brother into exile in 1721 and died there of a chronic illness. He was skilled in music and painting. The word in the text translated as graveyards, *pukmangsan*, occurs frequently in *shijo*. Originally it meant a mountain in China and referred to the place a person goes at death, a sort of underworld, but here it seems to mean simply graves or tombs.

280 (906)

If everyone were a government official,
would there be any farmers?
If doctors cured all disease, would graveyards be as they are?
Boy,
fill the glass to the brim; I'll live my life as I please.

## Chu Ŭishik (seventeenth, eighteenth century)

Chu Ŭishik was an official during the reign of Sukjong. A noted singer and painter, reputedly he had a very refined personality. Exact dates are not available.

281 (740)

Talkers are regarded as idle chatterers;
the silent are taken for fools.
The poor are scorned; the rich are envied.
I tell you,
talking is difficult under these skies.

## An Sŏu (1664–1735)

An Sŏu was a minor official during the reign of Sukjong. The road to preferment was blocked, prompting him to retire early and spend the rest of his life enjoying the simple delights of nature. "Blue mountains and green waters" is a traditional expression for the ideal life in nature. The reference is to the Analects 6.21 (translation by Arthur Waley): "The Master said, the wise man delights in water, the Good man delights in mountains. For the wise move; but the Good stay still. The wise are happy; but the Good, secure."

282 (2,064)

Why are blue mountains
ignorant like me?
Why are green waters insensible like me?
Do not mock
ignorance and insensibility; I'm going to enjoy these mountains
    and waters.

## Yun Tusŏ (1668–?)

Yun Tusŏ was the great-grandson of the illustrious poet Yun Sŏndo. Famous in his own right as a calligrapher and painter, reputedly he studied his subjects all day—he painted figures, animals, and plants—before trying to depict them in paint. The same eye for detail is evident in the only *shijo* attributed to him.

283 (1,527)

A mud-encrusted piece of jade
lies abandoned by the road.
People going, people coming all look on it as dirt.
So be it:
stay as you are, jade stone, someone who knows you will surely come.

## Kim Ch'ŏnt'aek (eighteenth century)

Precise dates are not available for Kim Ch'ŏnt'aek. We know that he was a contemporary and close friend of Kim Sujang, and that he was a considerable poet in his own right. In 1728 he compiled the first great *shijo* anthology, *Ch'ŏnggu yŏngŏn*. Although a minor official he seems to have preferred to spend his time savoring the finer things in life in the company of Kim Sujang's coterie. Many of his poems reflect his rejection of fame and honor, his preference for a life buried in nature with wine and song, and his respect for traditional Confucian morality. One gets the impression that poets like Kim Ch'ŏnt'aek, socially disadvantaged by not being *yangban*, compensated for this by rejecting advancement, by loading their poems with classical allusions, and by extolling the traditional Confucian virtues.

284 (1,775)

A good walker should not run;
a bad walker should not rest.
Please do not stop; prize the briefest moments.
To stop
on the way is worse than not to start at all.

285 (264)

> Scales judge the light and heavy;
> rulers judge the long and short.
> All things are thus;
> the heart alone
> is an exception: be careful now with this.

286 (107)

> Sober I drink again;
> drunk I lie down.
> Honor and dishonor are meaningless to me.
> I'll drink and drink,
> I'll drink a lifetime through; I'll never know a sober hour again.

287 (189)

> What is fame and honor?
> So much of life is sordid.
> Three cups of wine and a tune on the *kŏmun'go* are a day's work for me.
> In these fine
> peaceful times thus shall I grow old.

288 (84)

> If strong men fought
> over beautiful scenery,
> with my rank and power, how could I win my share?
> But no one
> really forbids, so I too will enjoy the scene.

289 (2,247)

> One with the setting sun the ibis flew,
> water and sky a single hue.
> I untied the skiff, got on board, rowed downstream to the narrows.
> On the other bank,
> a rain-hatted old man said: "Take me with you."

290 (2,374)

> White clouds and blue mist
> fill every mountain valley.

Leaves tinted by the autumn breeze are more beautiful
   than spring flowers.
God in heaven
has arranged these mountain hues just for my delight.

291 (27)

When autumn nights are very long,
thoughts of my love are even longer.
Sporadic rain falls on the paulownia, rotting what's left of my innards.
It seems
as if misfortune has been decreed for me alone.

292 (1,503)

I wake from a late afternoon nap
and open wine-drowsy eyes.
Flowers newly bloomed in the night rain give off a delicate fragrance.
Ah, how fresh
life is in this mountain dwelling!

293 (1,540)

I've taken off my clothes
and given them to the lad to pawn in the wine house.
I look up at the sky and ask the moon:
Is there any difference
between Li Bai of old and me today?

## Yun Sun (1680–1741)

Yun Sun served in a variety of positions under Sukjong and Yŏngjo. He was
a noted calligrapher.

294 (448)

My house is deep in White Crane Mountain;
who would wish to visit me here?
As guest I have the clear breeze; I have the bright moon to share a cup.
The crane maundering
in the corner of the yard is indeed my friend.

## Kim Sujang (1690–?)

Although Kim Sujang is one of the truly great *shijo* poets, very little is known about him. He was born in 1690; his family home was in Chŏnju; he served for an unspecified period of time as a minor official in the military ministry, a position not held by a *yangban*. Apart from these few documented facts, we know that he edited *Haedong kayo* (Songs of the Eastern Sea), the second great *shijo* anthology; that the process of editing and revising took about thirty years; that he built a villa called Nogajae on a mountain in Hwagae-dong in Seoul, where he spent an idyllic old age—he lived into his eighties—savoring the pleasures of nature and art in the company of his friends. One hundred and twenty-three of his *shijo* are extant. Kim Sujang broke new ground in *shijo* in terms of theme, language, and form. His love poems, in particular, reveal a new complexity of feeling, and his *sasŏl shijo* show the new *sŏmin* (common people) influence in the *shijo* form.

295 (2,121)

My straw-roofed hermitage is quite remote.
I sit alone; I have no friends.
White clouds doze naturally to the strains of a *shijo* song.
Does anyone
realize how fine this really is?

296 (587)

When autumn leaves are delicate reds
and the yellow chrysanthemum spews out its scent,
that's when the new season's wine matures and white-scaled fine raw
    fish have that special taste.
Boy,
bring out my *kŏmun'go*; I'll drink and sing alone.

297 (1,694)

I'm an old man now;
what are my interests?
The yellow chrysanthemum at the foot of the hedge, and the *kŏmun'go*
    on my desk.

In the midst of this,
my single music score is never idle.

298 (161)
There is reference here to a poem by Li Bai, *Chun ye yan tao li yuan xu.*

Flowers fall, spring passes;
the wine is all drunk, the mood comes on.
Time is a traveler that precipitates white hair.
Only senile
fools say, don't enjoy yourself while you may.

299 (131)
Kyŏnghoe Pavilion is in Kyŏngbok Palace. Inwangsan is the mountain behind the palace.

The pine forest at Kyŏnghoe Pavilion
stretches thickly before the eye;
the slopes of Inwang Mountain are a screen of flowering branches.
White herons
flap to and fro in the evening sun.

300 (2,091)
The *p'iri* is a Korean flute.

Clear autumn weather:
high into the Diamond Mountains I climb.
The boy on the *p'iri* and the singer with his song produce a new
    harmony of sound.
Cares lodged
so long in my heart all melt away.

301 (1,982)

The world is bright and buoyant;
the breeze is full of the joy of spring.
Peaches and pears are red and white; willows and orioles are
    yellow and green.
In this great age
of peace how can I avoid a party mood?

302 (927)
The Koryŏ Kingdom lasted from 918 to 1392.

> On steamy summer dog days
> I search out a cool clear valley,
> strip off, hang my clothes on a branch and sing an old Koryŏ song,
> thus to wash off
> in jade water the grime and dust that mires my body.

303 (536)

> This old sick heart
> I gave to the chrysanthemum;
> my skein of worries I gave to the dark grape,
> and to one long song
> I gave the white hair that streams beneath my ears.

304 (1,996)

> The talents heaven gave me have been of no avail;
> I have known neither honor nor disgrace.
> In the good times of the four seasons I have grown to be an old, white-
>      haired devotee of beauty.
> So be it:
> it's gone, it's gone. I'll enjoy myself as I please.

305 (428)

> Life here is so simple,
> all I have
> is a few grapevines and a single book of songs.
> Thus
> I place my trust in things that are beautiful.

306 (957)

> When the Great Dipper slips low in the sky
> and the Fifth Watch moves toward its close,
> I hear the sound of familiar footsteps; surely it is my love!
> Can gold express
> the joy of two smiling hearts each to each at that door?

307 (696)

The house behind is made of mud,
of wood the house next door;
My neighbors' clothes are woven from grass; berries and fruit are
 their store.
Those meat-eaters
who live in great houses, how can their hearts be so small?

308 (766)

The peony is the king of flowers,
the sunflower is a loyal, filial subject.
The plum is a recluse, the apricot a mean-spirited wretch. The lotus is
 a lady, the chrysanthemum a sage. The camellia is an indigent scholar,
 the gourd flower an old man. The China pink is a youth, the sea-rose
 a young girl.
Special among the flowers
is the pear blossom poet, while the red peach, the fairyland peach, and the
 three blossom peach all are devotees of beauty.

309 (2,120)

Between the twentieth day and the end of the month,
does any day preclude play?
In wind, rain, and snow I pass complaining days,
but when the moon
is bright and the wind is fresh, I never skip a day.

310 (2,344)

You who are drunk on bureaucratic ambition,
consider the future.
A naked child thinks only of the sunlight,
but when the sun
crosses west mountain, what's it going to do?

311 (2,330)

Hwagyedong was an area in Seoul.

> I've plaited a straw hut
> on the northern slope of Hwagyedong.
> Wind, rain, snow, and frost somehow I can endure,
> but when can I hope
> to bathe in the warmth of the sun?

312 (923)

> My belly filled with barley and rotten shad;
> that's a fine feeling.
> With a flourish of the brush I paint myself some grapes. Why
>     should I envy the Immortals?
> Such a fine life
> surely comes from the great favor of the king!

313 (1,434)

> Friends, let's go flower viewing;
> we'll fish the stream and have a picnic.
> Already it's too late to forbid the white locks beneath my ears.
> The road ahead,
> will it be long or short? That's something I just don't know.

314 (2,227)

Tao Qian (Tao Yuanming, 365–427) was a celebrated poet who lived in the Six Dynasties period in China.

> Trees and grasses wither
> when wind and frost are fused.
> White and yellow, the chrysanthemums are in full bloom.
> In our love
> for the chrysanthemum, is there any difference between Tao Yuanming
>     and me.

315 (1,073)

Segŏmjŏng, a pavilion in Seoul, was noted for its beauty. The military used the area for training and recreation.

We trained our army—center, right and left—
swept out the Northern Barbarian, swept out the Southern Scourge,
wiped our sullied swords and built Segŏmjŏng,
so that dignity
and virtue affirmed, peace might reign across the four seas.

316 (1,710)

For a long time now I've known
that life is but a dream.
With or without the wine jar, we'll enjoy everything that comes.
In this dusty world
it's hard to find lips parted in a smile. Let's enjoy ourselves all we can.

317 (193)

Confucius came into this world
so that Heaven might borrow his lips
to brighten into righteousness the darkness of human affairs.
Thus "heaven,"
"earth," and "man" are the finest characters drawn.

318 (486)

Green willows are good,
broad paulownias are better.
The patter of heavy rain on the paulownia tells the heart of the man:
long years spent
among the winds and frosts of time to become the five-string lute of
    Emperor Sun.

319 (540)

To say that growing old is sad
is the talk of a senile fool.
Heaven and earth have no limits; man's allotted span is a hundred years.
    All talk of sadness is the raving of a fool.
So be it:
what's the point in laughing at senility?

320 (178)

> You may extol fame and honor,
> but what about leisurely days?
> You may envy wealth and riches, but what about honest frugality?
> Between a hundred years
> of one and a hundred years of the other, is there really any difference?

321 (1,274)

> I'll take my cares
> and tie them tight.
> I'll plop them among blue waves and float them down the river.
> Drifting
> east and west, they'll disappear naturally.

322 (192)

> Virtue has lost its burnish
> since Confucius left the world.
> I sail the broad seas, but who will follow me?
> White gull,
> in leisure you and I are one: with you I'll cast my lot.

323 (2,242)

> Why is the sky round,
> why is the earth square?
> Who devised the principle of *yin* and *yang*?
> Presumably
> no one really knows the height of the sky or the breadth of the earth.

324 (2,013)

> Heaven and earth are parents;
> created things are wife and children.
> Rivers and mountains are brothers; breezes and moonlight are
>     close friends.
> In all this,
> have I ever forgotten the loyalty between ruler and subject?

325 (955)

> Father, to have given me life
> is favor of favors.
> Mother, to have reared me is virtue of virtues.
> How can I
> ever repay such heavenly largess?

326 (122)

> Black they say is white;
> white they say is black.
> Black or white, no one admits the fact.
> Better
> block my ears, close my eyes, refuse to listen, refuse to see.

327 (2,076)

The blue clouds refer to worldly ambition, the white clouds refer to the simple life in nature of the cultivated man.

> You may like blue clouds,
> but I like white clouds.
> You may enjoy riches and high station, but I like peace and frugality.
> Laugh, if you must,
> at what you consider folly, but how can I change?

328 (180)

> Set not your sights on fame and honor;
> be not swayed by rank and riches.
> Poverty and worldly success are in the hands of Heaven.
> A life
> devoted to virtue brings unending happiness.

329 (244)

> I have been unable to repay the favor of the king
> and now my parents are dead as well.
> Loyalty and filial piety are all in vain.
> So be it:
> I'll pass my remaining years in the spirit of the four seasons.

330 (1,922)

Moonlight shines on the lotus pond;
lotus fragrance pervades my clothes.
There's wine in the golden jug and a beauty playing the *kŏmun'go*.
　　Captivated by the mood I sing a sad refrain. Pine and bamboo sway
　　to my song; the cranes in the garden dance.
Thus,
　　happy with relatives, glad with friends, I'll live the span allotted me
　　by heaven.

331 (152)

Yuggak (six-sided) Pavilion on the slopes of Inwang Mountain in Seoul was
famous for its spring flower festival.

The flowers are about to bloom;
the willows are about to turn green.
The wine has matured; let's go, my friends.
We'll sit
in a circle in Yukkak Pavilion and greet the spring.

332 (929)

Fine morning after spring rain;
I awaken and get up.
Half-open buds battle to flower first.
Spring birds
captivated by the mood sing and dance.

333 (1,060)

Visitors never grace this mountain village,
and yet I am not lonely.
Flowers laugh, birds talk; leaves rustling in the bamboo grove provide
　　the sounds of conversation. The wind in the pines is the *kŏmun'go*,
　　while the cuckoo makes sweet song.
And there's no one
to flash an eye in envy of my riches.

334 (1,437)

> Folly, folly
> all is folly.
> To whom did I give my youth? Whose white hair is in my care?
> Search now
> though I may, there's nowhere to inquire.

335 (2,204)

> My hair may be white,
> but my heart is still green.
> Flowers can welcome me without any false pride.
> Girl,
> what have I done; why do you glare at me so?

336 (755)

> Drink or can't drink,
> never let the jug go empty;
> perform or can't perform, keep a beauty by your side.
> Thus you may
> console yourself for the fleeting pilgrim years.

337 (1,208)

The patterned skirt in this poem represents a moral judgment: a well-brought up young girl would not wear one.

> Look at that girl in blouse and patterned skirt,
> her face prettily powdered, her hair as yet unpinned.
> Yesterday she deceived me and now she's off to deceive another,
> fresh-cut flowers
> held firmly in her hand, hips swinging lightly as the sun goes down.

338 (325)

The magnet represents the male, the unthreaded needle the female. The disharmony is literally that which occurs when the *kŏmun'go* and *pip'a*, two traditional Korean musical instruments, are not in tune.

Perhaps I am a magnet
and girls are unthreaded needles.
Sit down and they cling to me; stand up and they follow. Lie down
    and they stick to me; bounce up and they don't fall off.
Husbands and wives
in marital disharmony, of magnet and needle compound a broth
    and drink it twice a day.

339 (822)

Of all the dogs around me, spotted, black, and hairy,
    that yellow bitch is certainly by far the most frustrating.
In sheer delight she runs to welcome those whom I despise, while those
    I like she barks at, rooting them outside.
The next dog-monger
who passes by my gate will get that bitch trussed tightly, abandoned
    to her fate.

340 (72)

Ah, the variety
of the female species!
Falcons; swallows perched on a line; herons on a hundred flowers;
    ducks on blue waters, great and small; hawks sitting quietly
    on the ground; owls in rotten trees.
But all are beauties,
for all are loved by men.

341 (1,831)

Within the higher ranks of the military office
whether my name is known I cannot say,
    but, believe me when I tell you, that old though I may be,
        I still can dance and sing, and I never miss an outing,
        wherever it may be. As for the flower and willow
        world, there's nowhere I haven't been.

So, girls,
when you despise a man like me, know that you slight one who
    were he granted a single night of love, might well become
    the lion among your lover hordes.

### 342 (227)

Eat, she says, her rotten bean-curd pancakes, fried in cold water,
a man like me who wouldn't eat the richest rice-cakes to be had!
Marry her, she says, the noseless hag, a man like me who wouldn't marry
    the finest beauty in the land!
Except for that spouse
ordained by heaven, how can I have eyes for any woman?

### 343 (1,035)

Listen to me, girl,
you're wasted as a head-shorn nun.
You'll spend your life reciting sutras in dark, lonely worship-halls. And
    when you die, you'll be laid in a wicker coffin, chin propped with a
    fuller's stick. And when the ashes of the fire turn cold, you'll be a
    spirit crying in the bitter rain of a bare, exposed mountain.
But should you
change your mind and surround yourself with descendants, running,
    crawling, like lice in matted hair, you might, perhaps, think twice
    about one hundred years of worldly pleasure.

### 344 (1,689)

The trials and tribulations of this life
I'll write in detail on a shield-shaped kite.
On the fifteenth of January, when the west wind blows strong, I'll reel
    out the line and hoist it aloft. One last, parting cup I'll drink, then
    let it go free, shooting, soaring, higher, still higher, wriggling, weaving,
    like the White Dragon seething, till it disappears in the clouds or
    crosses the Eastern Sea, to be caught in the branches of a solitary tree,
there to fade
into nothingness in gentle rain and softly blowing breeze.

## Kim Ugyu (1691–?)

Kim Ugyu was a singer during the reign of Yŏngjo. He was a friend of Kim Sujang, learned his singing from Pak Sanggŏn, and afterwards achieved fame himself as a singer.

345 (537)

> Old and sick,
> my household sunk in poverty, I have no friends.
> When I lived well, many came and went.
> Now my best friend
> is a three-foot stick cut from a goosefoot.

346 (102)

> Rain clears on rivers and streams;
> water and sky are the same color.
> I load the wine in my tiny boat; rod across my shoulder I drift
>     downstream.
> The white gulls
> in the rushes are delighted to see me.

347 (1,337)

> I urge the children to hurry up.
> They finish eating; I take them with me.
> We find a place on the paddy field dike, lie down, pillow on sheaves.
> Beside us,
> a like-minded friend suggests a game of chess.

## Yi Chŏngbo (1693–1766)

Yi Chŏngbo, a scholar-official, is the representative *yangban* (nobleman) *shijo* poet of the reign of Yŏngjo, an era when many of the finest poets belonged to the *chungin* (neither *yangban* nor commoner) class. An official who held many posts in the course of a long career, he was noted for his upright character and his fearlessness in the cause of right; he did not hesitate to send memorials to the throne that were critical of government policies. He is said to have written most of his *shijo* poems in old age after he had retired to the

countryside. His poems reflect typical upper-class preoccupations along with
a new awareness of the common man, presumably the result of his familiar-
ity with *Shirhak*, or Practical Learning.

348 (1,037)

> Spring visits a farming household;
> life gets naturally busy:
> fish-pots to lay in the stream in front, cucumber seeds to sow beneath
>     the paling.
> Tomorrow,
> if the clouds clear off, I'll go and dig mountain herbs.

349 (166)

> When flowers bloom, I think of the moon;
> when the moon is bright, I think of wine;
> when flowers bloom, and the moon is bright, and I have some wine,
>     I think of a friend.
> When shall I sit
> with a friend beneath the flowers, enjoy the moon, and drink the long
>     night through.

350 (930)

> Why do grasses and trees
> delight in spring?
> Why do grasses wither and leaves fall in autumn?
> Pine and bamboo,
> green all the year round, I envy you.

351 (1,001)

> Can an old man
> become young again?
> Can lost teeth spring back, white hair turn black?
> Sad to say
> there's no elixir in this life.

352 (362)

> The sun that sets beyond west mountain
> rises again in the East Sea;
> The grasses that wither in the fall grow green again in the spring.
> Why is it
> that human life, nature's noblest creation, goes and never returns?

353 (562)

> Can medicine cure a sickness
> that comes from love's yearning?
> Awake or asleep, sighs and tears weigh me down.
> Forget I shan't,
> this side of the grave.

354 (26)

> Like a lotus blossom
> half open in bright autumn moonlight;
> like a sea rose dozing in fine rain on an easterly breeze;
> perfect beauty
> like this, I presume, belongs to you alone.

355 (252)

> I lay my head on the pillow
> to summon my love in dreams.
> The lamp on the wall is growing dim; it's cold beneath the duck-
>     embroidered quilt;
> the honk of
> a lone goose in the night keeps me from sleep.

356 (1,441)

> Lord of creation,
> there is no justice.
> Swallows and butterflies, kingfishers and mandarin ducks, all are paired!
> Why, then,
> must this poor body live all alone?

357 (64)

> I'll never forget the boy
> who slept here last night.

He could be the son of a tile-maker the way clay yields to his touch,
    or the scion of a mole the way he burrows and thrusts, or perhaps
    the stripling of a seaman the way the oar answers his pulse. His first
    experience, he avows, a claim that raises certain doubts.
I've had my share
before and I assume I'll have some more, but the memory of that boy last
    night is a pleasure I shall always store.

### 358 (98)

"Rivers and streams" translates *kangho*, a reference to the district in China that boasts three rivers and five lakes, with the secondary meaning of the secluded world of the hermit.

Do not envy the joy of fish
playing in rivers and streams.
When the fishermen go home, white egrets stalk their prey.
All day long
fish dash and dive: no time for ease or rest.

### 359 (2,216)

All my life I've wished
my body could sprout wings,
soar into the blue sky and scatter those clouds,
thus to stop them
from ever again screening the bright sun and moon.

### 360 (805)

Tiger moth, let me ask you a question.
I cannot understand you at all.
One moth dies, yet the next insists on following.
A worthless
insect you may be, but why are you ignorant of death?

### 361 (1,189)

A blind man on a purblind horse
rode off into the night.
That blind man fell into the water crossing a wide river.
Had he never attempted
the crossing, would he have fallen off?

362 (210)

A pear blossom trembles in a crazy wind;
it flies here, it flies there.
Unable to mount a tree branch, it gets caught in a spider's web.
The spider
spins its web, thinking the captive petal a butterfly.

363 (505)

Who can build a fine big house
in a brief span of time
to look after the poor, weak scholars of the world?
The good will
I applaud, but for ineffectual resolve, is there any difference
between you and me?

364 (569)

Would that my love were a paulownia tree
and I an arrowroot vine in spring.
I'd bind her around as the spider spirals a butterfly, tightly this way,
tightly that. Where the thread went wrong, I'd unravel it and wind
it right. Where it twisted and tangled, I'd straighten it out, bottom
to top, leaving nothing to chance, tightly, tightly, round and round,
night and day, tightly bound.
Midwinter
wind, rain, snow, and frost, let them buffet as they will: they'll never
topple my paulownia tree.

365 (1,771)

Yesterday a flower bloomed;
and a flower bloomed today.
Today's flower is in full bloom; yesterday's flower is already old.
Flowers age,
men age, too: let's enjoy ourselves while we may.

## Cho Myŏngni (1697–1756)

Cho Myŏngni had a checkered career in the bureaucracy. Having served in various positions, his recommendation of Yi T'aejung for a position in the Royal Archives caused a controversy that led to dismissal and exile. Restored to office in 1739, he served in a number of high ministerial offices.

366 (304)

> The wild geese have all flown off;
> frost follows frost.
> Autumn nights are long; sad thoughts fill my heart.
> Bright moonlight
> bathes the yard by night: it's just like home.

367 (1,147)
The poet puns on the winter and autumn names for the Diamond Mountains.

> On my way to Sŏraksan
> I met a Diamond Mountain monk.
> I asked: what's the mountain like this fall?
> Recently,
> he said, there's been a lot of frost; you've come at the perfect time.

## Yi Chae (1725–76)

Yi Chae was a scholar-official during the reign of Yŏngjo. His *shijo* are optimistic songs, singing of the simple delights of nature.

368 (1,106)

> The morning star has set; the lark is on the wing.
> Hoe on shoulder, I open the brushwood gate.
> The chill dew on the long grass soon wets my hemp breeches.
> Boy,
> if times are good, what matter if our clothes get wet?

## Hwang Yunsŏk (1729–91)

Hwang Yunsŏk was a scholar-official who served under Yŏngjo and Chŏngjo. He was a special assistant to Yŏngjo.

369 (Shim 380)

Wild beasts know cold and warmth,
wild beasts know hunger and plenty.
Could they be unaware of life and death, gain and loss?
How sad!
Don't say wild beasts are base. Look rather to yourself as noble.

## Shin Hŏnjo (1752–1807)

Shin Hŏnjo is one of the poets whose work has only recently been discovered. His achievement awaits critical appraisal.

370 (Shim 1,709)

Boy, don't drive the crows
from the forest.
The insignificant also repay their parents' favor.
Orphaned
as I am, I envy them.

## Shin Wi (1769–1847)

An official during the reign of Chŏngjo, Shin Wi was skilled in the three traditional divisions of art: poetry, calligraphy, and painting. Kwandong refers to the scenic area on the east coast, stretching from Uljin to Wonsan. Myŏngsashimni (literally "ten *li* of shining sand) is a beach outside Wonsan famous for the sea-roses that bloom in profusion there.

371 (807)
This poem is sometimes ascribed to Songch'ung (?–656), a Paekche official.

Tell me, reverend sir,
how was the scenery in Kwandong?
Sea-roses were red across the sands of Myŏngsashimni,
and near the distant
water's edge, paired white gulls flew through desultory rain.

## Pak Hyogwan (*1781–1880*)

In 1876, in collaboration with his pupil An Minyŏng, Pak Hyogwan compiled the third famous *shijo* anthology, *Kagok wŏllyu*. He spent his life savoring the delights of music, wine, and song and lived to extreme old age. His poems sing of the transience of human existence, the sorrows of love, and devotion to the precepts of Confucian morality.

372 (524)

> Who says the crow
> is black and ugly?
> With tasty morsels the grown chick repays its mother's favors. Is not this
> the mark of beauty?
> How sad to think
> man cannot emulate that bird.

373 (2,222)

> I wished to sweep away the clouds that blot the sun,
> to see an age of peace ensue,
> but my galloping horse stopped and aged, my keen sword rusted
> and tarnished.
> White hair importunes
> as time goes by; I cannot curb my indignation.

374 (1,182)

> Time flows like water;
> suddenly it's spring again.
> New vegetables in old fields, brilliant flowers on old trees.
> Boy,
> lay out new wine; we'll celebrate the new spring.

375 (2,162)

> To become a tiger butterfly
> in spring breezes, bright sun, and good times;
> to sport, drenched in the scent of a hundred varieties of flowers!
> In this world
> what could compare with such a delectable tingle?

376 (1,117)

Wild goose crying as you fly
through frost and star-sparse sky,
how urgent your flight surging through the night?
Fear, perhaps,
of being late for some tryst in the south?

377 (198)

Cuckoo, crying on the bare mountain,
why such bitter tears?
Have you, like me, experienced parting?
Cry you may
until you bleed, but do you get an answer?

## Kim Samhyŏn (eighteenth century)

Precise dates are not available for Kim Samhyŏn, a general during the reign
of Sukjong. After retiring from public service, he devoted himself to the
beauties of nature. His songs are cheerful and optimistic.

378 (440)

My soul I'll mingle with wine;
I'll flow inside my love.
Through tortuous intestinal trails the search may lead,
but I'll sweep
clean forever the heart that left me for another.

379 (183)

Do not exult over fame,
for half is honor and half dishonor.
Do not covet riches or high station, for this is to step on perilous paths.
Leisure is
what we're about; we have nothing to fear.

## Songgyeyŏnwŏl (eighteenth century)

Songgyeyŏnwŏl was a singer during the reign of Yŏngjo. Precise dates are not available.

380 (116)

> Fingers reached to strum the *kŏmun'go*,
> but soreness kept them still.
> I hung it in the shade of the pines that stand at my north window.
> Now the song
> of the strings in the wind, that indeed is something to hear.

381 (1,203)

> When I was young and fearless
> I set my heart on fame and honor.
> In middle years I learned that ambition is a floating cloud.
> A house beneath
> a pine, a *kŏmun'go*, and a book—these are the things that befit my station.

382 (715)
Mach'ŏn Pass is in Hamgyŏng Province in North Korea.

> Sitting on top of Mach'ŏn Pass
> I look down at the East Sea.
> Beyond the water I see the clouds, beyond the clouds the sky.
> Ah, this is a sight
> I could look at all the days of my life!

383 (1,069)
The Third Watch was the hour immediately before and after midnight.

> The moon rises in the Third Watch;
> the shadow of a pine is on my window.
> Good things taste better at this hour.
> I ask you:
> those drunk on this red, dusty world, are they asleep or awake?

### *Kim Chint'ae (eighteenth century)*

Precise dates are not available for Kim Chint'ae, a singer during the reign of Yŏngjo.

384 (1,862)

> Listen to me, lad. Don't be proud
> of your youthful looks.
> Time is fleet; black shining hair soon turns white.
> We, too,
> believed in youth: we have learned nothing.

385 (2,220)

> You ask what I
> most want in life?
> A phoenix-like pen and the statecraft of the spider.
> Phoenix and spider,
> you don't need these skills; how about giving them to me?

386 (2,250)

> Summer clouds, masses of mystery peaks;
> are the Diamond Mountains thus?
> Jade-like lotus flowers right in front of my eyes.
> I suppose
> I'm sad because I cannot climb up there.

387 (1,565)

Sŏng Sammun was one of the Six Martyred Subjects executed for being implicated in the plot to restore Tanjong to the throne.

> Dragon-like spreading pine,
> I'm glad, so glad.
> Tried by thunder, by lightning, yet you stay so green?
> Who says
> Sŏng Sammun is dead? It's as if I see him now.

## Kim Sŏnggi (*eighteenth century*)

Precise dates are not available for Kim Sŏnggi. He was a singer during the reign of Yŏngjo, and he was skilled both in the *kŏmun'go* and the bamboo flute. Originally he was an archer, but he gave up archery for music. His poems sing of the delights of nature. "Rivers and lakes"—*kangho*—once again refers to Du Fu's five rivers and three lakes, with the secondary meaning of the hermit's abode.

### 388 (99)

The man who abandons himself to rivers and lakes
befriends the white gull,
drifts on a skiff and plays the jade flute loud.
Doubtless
these are the ultimate pleasures in life.

### 389 (1,671)

With nothing to do,
I go to West Lake.
White gulls crowd the skies above white sands and clear waters.
From somewhere
a fisherman's song helps the mood.

### 390 (1,521)

I cut a branch from the plum
planted in the jade pot.
The flower is beautiful, the fragrance even better.
So be it:
the flower is cut, but I can't throw it away?

### 391 (2,327)

I shake off all the dust of the world,
take out my bamboo stick, don my straw sandals.
Soon I reach a scenic mountain spot, my *kŏmun'go* slung across my back.
The cry of a crane
that has lost its mate echoes from the clouds.

## Kim Yŏng (eighteenth century)

Kim Yŏng was an official during the reign of Chŏngjo.

392 (978)

> White heron, standing on that empty boat,
> are you white because washed in blue waves?
> Body so white, is your heart white, too?
> If your heart
> is like your body, I will surely play with you.

## Yi Chŏngjin (eighteenth century)

Precise dates are not available for Yi Chŏngjin. He was a singer and an official, a county chief apparently, during the reign of Yŏngjo.

393 (2,094)

> The mirror I looked at in youth
> I look at again in white-haired old age.
> Youth has gone; it is no more: all I see is white hair.
> White hair,
> did youth go freely? I think you drove it out.

394 (260)

"No sign of crab or net" is an idiomatic way of saying someone has vanished without trace.

> Dream, you brought my love from afar.
> You brought him just for me.
> So glad I was, I woke from sleep and rose up from my bed.
> But my love
> must have left in anger, for there was no sign of crab or net.

395 (857)

This poem depicts the predatory nature of human society, punning on the word for "child" and "dragonfly."

> Naked children waving spider sticks
> run to and from the stream.
> "Dragonfly, dragonfly," they cry. "Fly that way and die, fly this way
>     and live."

I suppose
all the affairs of the world are thus.

396 (1,904)

> Death may be a bitter pill,
> but growing old is bitterer still.
> Arms heavy in dance, breath short in song.
> And to cap it all,
> not up to wine or women; that's really sore.

## Kim Yugi (eighteenth century)

Kim Yugi was a singer during the reign of Sukjong.

397 (2,157)

> Peach blossoms in the spring breeze,
> do not boast of your beauty.
> Consider the spreading pine and the green bamboo at year's end.
> What can change
> the heart that's truly noble?

## Kim Sŏngch'oe (eighteenth century)

Kim Sŏngch'oe, grandson of Kim Kwang'uk, was an official during the reign of Sukjong.

398 (1,238)

> Wine drowsiness wears thin;
> I sit up and play the *kŏmun'go*.
> A crane outside the window dances for joy.
> Boy,
> pour the rest of the wine; the mood is coming again.

## An Minyŏng (1816–95)

An Minyŏng was one of the last great *shijo* poets. He belongs in the tradition of poets who devoted themselves to the simple delights of nature. Although he had friends in high places, notably the regent T'aewŏn'gun, he was blocked from preferment by his non-*yangban* status. In 1876, in collaboration with his teacher Pak Hyogwan, he compiled the third great *shijo* anthology *Kagok wŏllyu.*

A very large number of An Minyŏng poems have been discovered in recent times. These poems await detailed scholarly evaluation. However, it is safe to number him among the great exponents of *shijo*. Perhaps his most acclaimed poems are in the *Song of the Plum* series, eight poems composed on the occasion of a party in the mountain home of his teacher, Pak Hyogwan, in praise of a plum that Pak had cultivated. The series is translated below, poems 404–11.

399 (606)

> Flowers bloom within the fence;
> willows line the edge of the pond.
> The oriole sings; the butterfly dances.
> Flowers red,
> willows green, orioles singing, and butterflies dancing; I'll enjoy myself
>     until I'm drunk.

400 (655)

> Peach blossoms fly in the air,
> greenness spreads around.
> The song of the oriole rolls through the misting rain.
> As I offer
> the wine cup, a lady, delicately made up, graces the scene.

401 (500)

> High or low,
> far or near,
> square or circular, long or short:
> this is my life;
> I have no worries.

402 (202)

> Traveler, returning in the night
> through bare mountain's snowy blast,
> the dog is barking at the gate; can you hear it, can you not?
> Snow covers
> the narrow stony path; lay down your donkey's reins.

403 (1,781)

The clouds have been swept
across the width of the sky.
Round and high, how brightly you shine in the center of the sky!
I know why:
tonight is the January full moon in a great reign of peace.

*Song of the Plum*

404 (520)

You have indeed bloomed
in fulfillment of your snow pledge.
The moon rises in the gloaming: shadows appear.
Clear fragrance
floats in the cup: I'll enjoy myself till I'm drunk.

405 (1,383)
"Delicate fragrance wafts through the air" is a quotation from the Song dynasty poet Lin Bu.

I didn't believe you
on that weak, scraggy branch.
You've kept your snow pledge: two, three flowers have bloomed.
Candle in hand,
I approach in admiration: a delicate fragrance wafts through the air.

406 (992)

Ice crystal, jade bead,
that's you in the snow,
gently loosing your fragrance in tryst with the twilight moon.
For elegance
and nobility of spirit, you stand alone.

407 (2,301)

The sun goes down; the moon rises.
Was it so pledged with you?
Flowers asleep in the bedroom release a fragrant greeting.
Plum and moon
are friends: why didn't I know?

408 (743)

> Plum shadows hit the window,
> hit the slanted gold pin in a beauty's hair.
> Two or three white-haired old men enjoy the *kŏmun'go* and a song.
> And when they pass
> the wine cup around, the moon rises too.

409 (1,847)
Luofu shan is a mountain in China famous for its plum blossoms.

> Gnarled old stump, black and craggy,
> sticking from the snows of Luofu shan.
> By what green force have your branches burgeoned, blossoming
>      into flower?
> The boat may be
> rotten, but even with half a boat, I cannot resist the will of spring.

410 (660)

> Those flowers hidden in East Pavilion,
> are they rhododendrons or azaleas?
> The whole world is snow; they wouldn't dare bloom.
> Now I understand:
> only the plum blooms when snowflakes fly in early spring.

411 (836)

> The wind drives the snow;
> it strikes the window of this mountain villa.
> Gelid air seeps through and attacks the sleeping plum.
> Let the air
> freeze all it wishes; can it filch the will of spring?

## *Yi Sebo (1832–95)*

Yi Sebo is among the last of the great *shijo* poets. A huge number of his *shijo* were discovered in recent years, giving him the distinction of having the most extant poems in the history of the genre. These poems were not available when Chŏng Pyŏng'uk and Shim Chaewan published their collections. They are, however, in Pak Ŭlsu's *Han'guk shijo taesajŏn* (1992). Yi Sebo's *shijo* await critical evaluation, but from the few poems translated below, it is evident that he is a major poet. *P'unga*, the songbook compiled by Yi Sebo, uses the *shijo-ch'ang,* but his poems are also in *Kagok wŏllyu.* On that basis and also for the sake of uniformity, the translations use the five-line format of the *kagok-ch'ang.*

412 (Pak 4,687)

> Orioles have willows;
> butterflies have flowers.
> Geese have blue waters; white cranes have green pines.
> How come a man
> has nowhere to place his trust.

413 (Pak 4,662)

> Spring comes to the garden;
> shrubs in flower take my breath away.
> Lovely, lovely! I cut some and return to my humble home.
> In all this
> why try to describe infinite joy?

414 (Pak 4,666)

> Were it not for coming together in the bridal,
> would we have shared our trust?
> Were it not for affection through rising sun and setting moon would we
>     have any joy?
> One fault:
> how could it get us in such a mess.

415 (Pak 4,632)

> I've lost youth's rose cheeks;
> I mourn my hoary hair.
> Youth is irretrievable; it's useless to grieve for what's over and done.
> Somehow
> a callow youth never knows what's to come!

416 (Pak 4,717)

> A fire starts in the heart;
> who will put it out?
> If no fire is impervious to water,
> how come
> water won't quench the fire of love?

417 (Pak 4502)

> One sea is hard enough;
> but blocked by three!
> Waves crash, winds howl.
> Back and forward,
> I keep searching for the shore.

## Yi Chaemyŏn (1845–1912)

Yi Chaemyŏn was the eldest son of Taewŏn'gun. The Cloud Terrace was in the Southern Palace of the Han dynasty.

418 (2,317)

> That old man is a free spirit,
> a devotee of wine and song;
> a scholarly figure, mind you, elegant and refined, with a face like an
>     Immortal in an old, exotic painting.
> I asked him:
> How many years since first you secluded yourself in the Cloud Terrace?

## Cho Hwang (nineteenth century)

Very little is known about Cho Hwang other than that he lived during the reign of Sunjo. His poems have only recently been discovered, and his achievement awaits critical appraisal. The three examples quoted here show that he possessed an original imagination.

419 (Shim 308)

> Deep in a valley of Nine Crane Mountain
> I follow the peach blossoms and flowing waters.
> So quiet and peaceful: this beautiful place must surely be the home
>     of the Immortals.
> So be it.
> I'll spend the time remaining to me in this life in wine's rapture.

420 (Shim 1,686)

> The crane sleeping on the pine altar
> was wakened by the onset of wind and frost.

Up it swooshed beneath the moon; ninety thousand *li* the road opened
    in front.
Crane,
lend me your wings; let me sport through the universe.

421 (Shim 888)

Peach and plum in the east garden,
in your glory place no trust.
When all your blooming's done, what about a night of wind and rain?
Think, then,
of yesterday: was it not an empty dream?

## Ch'oe Chikt'ae (*unidentified*)

422 (2,246)

If every day could count for
two, three months by ten,
trysts with my love, of course, would be more frequent,
but nature
arbitrarily decrees otherwise; this saddens my heart.

## Na Chisŏng (*unidentified*)

423 (290)

The moon that fades at the end of the month
brightens again on the fifteenth night.
The flowers that fall this year bloom again next spring.
So be it:
I look forward to new moons and fresh flowers.

## Yi Chungjip (*unidentified*)

424 (525)

Who says I am old?
does an old man act like this?
The sight of flowers delights me; a cup of wine brings a grin to my face.
As for white hair
streaming in the wind, what can I do about it?

## An Yŏnbo (unidentified)

425 (272)

Longing that leads to lovesickness; that's a thrill.
Lovesickness and a love tryst; that's a thrill.
I enjoy myself, then parting comes; even that's a thrill.
A lifetime
without such thrills! Would living be any fun?

## Ho Sŏkkyun (unidentified)

426 (2,135)

That boat floating on the autumn river,
whither is it bound?
We'll climb aboard her snow-bright moonlight load.
Near and far
irrelevant, we'll go wherever the mood takes us.

427 (251)

I lay down to sleep that in dreams
at least I might see my love.
But the cuckoo cried till the moon went down; what could I do?
So be it:
In terms of heart-rending yearning, are you and I any different?

## Yi P'ansŏ In'ŭng (unidentified)

428 (168)

How could the heart that loved the flower
know that one day the flower would fall,
or that love so sweet in candlelight would end in parting?
Why is nature
so unchanging while the human heart keeps changing day by day?

## Kim Ch'iu (*unidentified*)

429 (91)

> River village men with nets on your shoulders,
> do not trap the wild goose.
> For who will carry news from the frozen north to the rivers of the south?
> Fishermen
> from the river village you may be, but does this preclude all parting?

## Kim Hag'yŏn (*unidentified*)

430 (914)

> Blue-cloud skies, yellow-blossom earth;
> west wind urgent as the geese fly from the north.
> I stand here in the gelid dawn wondering who brought the wine blush
>     to frosted trees in a single night.
> Doubtless,
> tears of bitter parting have dyed the world thus.

## Ha Sunil (*unidentified*)

431 (149)

> Lovely the lotus;
> how mysterious your fragrance!
> Elegantly attired, a delight to so many!
> Surely
> you are the prince of flowers!

## Kwŏn Ingnyung

Precise dates are not available for Kwŏn Ingnyung. He was an official and eventually attained the rank of governor. The ascription of the poem is doubtful.

432 (69)

> Has the dew on the withered leaves
> already turned to frost?
> Autumn waters are broad and placid; old thoughts revive in my heart.
> Boy,
> raise the sail, push off the boat; we'll go and find a friend.

## Ch'ŏn'gŭm

Nothing is known of Ch'ŏn'gŭm except that she was a *kisaeng*.

433 (1,062)

> Night comes to a mountain village;
> a dog barks in the distance.
> I open the brushwood gate; the sky is cold, the moon is up.
> Listen, doggie:
> the moon's asleep on the bare mountain; what's the point in barking?

## Maehwa

Maehwa was a *kisaeng* in P'yŏngyang. Precise dates are not available. Maehwa, a typical *kisaeng* name, means "plum." The poem is obviously allegorical, with the stump of the plum referring to Maehwa herself, and the spring snow variously interpreted as a reference to a rival or to her own whitening hair.

434 (746)

> Spring returns
> to an old plum stump;
> it's time for flowers to bloom on customed branches.
> Spring snow, though,
> so wildly blows, I know not if flowers will grow.

## Hongjang

Hongjang was a *kisaeng* in Kangnŭng. Precise dates are not available. Han-
sŏng (Cold Pine) Pavilion and Kyŏngp'o Lookout are in Kangnŭng.

435 (2,271)

> The moon is bright over Hansŏng Pavilion,
> the water off Kyŏngp'o Lookout is calm.
> Seagulls are dependable: they fly over and back.
> Why is it
> my prince has gone and doesn't return?

## Chin'ok

Chin'ok was a *kisaeng*. No dates are available.

436 (2,032)

> Metal I thought, yes,
> but metal of an inferior kind.
> Now I see it's metal of the purest mint.
> I have
> a bellows: I think I ought to melt it down.

# PART IV

*Anonymous Songs*

# PART IV

## *Anonymous Songs*

The term *shijo* immediately brings to mind the names of the great *shijo* poets—Chŏng Ch'ŏl, Yun Sŏndo, and Kim Sujang, to name but a few. However, approximately half the extant canon of *shijo* poetry is the work of anonymous poets, most of whom wrote no earlier than the beginning of the eighteenth century. At least, there is great difficulty in proving earlier authorship since the earliest of the great *shijo* anthologies, *Ch'ŏnggu yŏng'ŏn*, appeared in 1728.

During the seventeenth century, *Shirhak* (Practical Learning), with its emphasis on empirical knowledge and practical living, came to prominence. With it came a movement away from poetry to prose as the mode of literary expression and a consequent emphasis on realism. This new emphasis had a reverse influence on the writing of poetry and meant, in effect, an expansion in the range of *shijo* poetry. Hitherto, *shijo* had been very much a poetry of the *yangban's* study and garden or, if it left these confines, the landscapes of great nature—mountain valleys, rivers, and lakes. The new emphasis on realism took *shijo* out of this narrow environment into the broader world of the quotidian. Instead of dealing only with Confucian values and the harmony between man and nature—although such themes continued to be treated—poetry, for the first time, began to deal with themes from the everyday lives of the people. *Shijo* left the *yangban's* study and entered the ordinary man's kitchen and backyard. Themes traditionally taboo suddenly began to be treated, for example, relations between the sexes and sex itself, and poets did not hesitate to use frank and forthright language quite outside the traditional ambiance of *shijo*. This gave *shijo* both an immediacy and relevance that it had not hitherto possessed and the characteristic sense of wry humor that has distinguished the form ever since.

## *Moral Songs*

The moral poems in particular reveal the humor that is so much a part of the anonymous *shijo* tradition: they are filled with toads, fleas, and a variety of incapacitated animals; they poke fun at *yangban* society, they satirize the bureaucracy and the religious world; and in the process they inculcate a native earthy wisdom.

### 437 (1,413)

This allegory deplores the evils perpetrated by corrupt officials, the lack of enlightened leadership, and the consequent sacrifice of the innocent. The Chinese characters literally read "the sound of trees falling," but Korean commentators interpret them as "the sound of leaves falling."

> What manner of grub has eaten
> the great spreading pines?
> Where has the long-beaked woodpecker gone?
> The sound of leaves
> falling on the naked mountain gives my heart no rest.

### 438 (156)

In this political allegory, the birds represent fair-minded men, the flowers young blameless officials, and the wind a political event that has been the downfall of these young officials.

> Birds, don't be sad
> that the flowers are falling.
> The wind sweeps them in flight; it's not their fault.
> When spring shouts
> a taunting goodbye, is there any point in envy?

### 439 (1,240)

The pardon referred to here is the type of amnesty proclaimed on auspicious occasions, such as a royal wedding or birth.

> A concubine with wine, but who won't give me any,
> a wife who is jealous because I have a concubine!
> I'll abduct them both and exile them to Cheju Island.

Twelve royal pardons
in the space of a year will not suffice to free them.

440 (2,257)

A toad, blind in one eye,
and dragging one leg,
intent on catching a lame, frostbitten fly, jumped but flopped flat on
    its back.
Fortunately,
it was quick to react: had it been slow, it might have bled to death.

441 (1,915)
Buddhist monks and nuns have closely shaved heads. A *kut* is a shamanistic
ritual.

The monk grabbed the nun by her hair;
the nun gripped the monk by his topknot.
Grappled thus, they fought, each claiming the other wrong, while a bevy
    of blind men watched the *kut*.
Meanwhile,
deaf mutes judged the rights and wrongs.

442 (1,382)

If a fool, a complete fool;
if mad, stark, raving mad.
A fool? Perhaps. A madman? Maybe. Knowing? Maybe. Ignorant?
    Perhaps.
Confusion
upon confusion; I cannot unravel the facts.

443 (1,334)

When I was a child I'd clap my hands
and follow the blind around.
Now when I think of it, the blind are better off than me.
If it weren't
for these damn eyes, would my insides fester so?

444 (1,539)

> I want to do what is right;
> who will say it is right now?
> I want to do what is wrong; who will say it is right afterwards?
> To get drunk
> and not distinguish right from wrong is the right thing to do.

445 (62)

This poem is interpreted variously as a political allegory declaring that those who fall from grace in a political upheaval may be reinstated one day or as a moral poem indicating the vanity of power and those who hold it, the speed at which the eyes of the world change when power changes hands, and the need for a vibrant humanity in the human situation.

> The peach blossoms filling the garden
> fell in the wind that blew last night.
> The boy takes the broom; he's going to sweep them up.
> Are fallen flowers
> any the less flowers; why not leave them unswept?

446 (1,188)

> A blind man carried
> a blind man on his back.
> Without supports on his clogs, or stockings on his feet, or a stick in his
>       hand, he inched across a rotten, single-log bridge.
> A stone Buddha,
> standing beneath, guffawed at the sky.

447 (1,212)

> On the road that twists beneath the pines,
> three monks are walking in a line.
> "Rear monk," I cry, "the Buddha who made human parting, who makes
>       men live alone, sleep alone, in what temple is he to be found?"
> "I do not know,"
> rear monk replies, "but our head monk's sister knows!"

448 (632)

Between heaven and earth
there's nothing a worthy man can do?
Study letters? Learning is the beginning of all worry. Take the sword?
    Military skill is a lethal blade.
Better spend my time
flitting between wine and *kisaeng* houses.

449 (247)

The story is told that in old China a high official sat one day with the king watching insects being caught in a spider's web. Suddenly it occurred to him that position was man's spider's web, whereupon he resigned his post and returned home to obscurity.

Grub to cicada,
sprout wings and away you fly.
How sweet your song on the top of a lofty tree!
Beware!
a spider's web lurks up there.

450 (2,024)

I'll gather all the sharp blades under heaven;
with them I'll make a broom.
And when I've swept out the Southern Barbarian and the Northern
    Scourge,
I'll take the metal,
fashion a hoe, and weed my fields along the riverbank.

451 (2,158)

This poem may be interpreted as a political allegory or as an illustration of a simple truth in nature and human life. Yi Chŏngbo has a very similar poem (see no. 362, p. 136).

A plum petal falls in the spring breeze;
it flies here, it flies there.
Unable to mount a tree, look, it's caught in a spider's web.
That spider
spins its web, twining the captive petal as it would a butterfly.

452 (2,295)

> The sun had all gone down
> when I lost my unbridled cow.
> I plucked some grass, held it in my hand, and tried to track the cow,
> but fog fell
> thick in the valley; I had no idea where it had gone.

453 (184)

> I sought fame and honor:
> everyone dislikes me.
> Surely childhood friends will not abandon me?
> Boy,
> prepare for a journey; today we're going home.

454 (739)

> Don't talk about others
> just for the pleasure of talking.
> If I talk about others, others will talk about me.
> Talk leads to talk:
> better be unable to talk at all.

455 (Shim 30)

> If I laugh to myself,
> I'm small-minded;
> If I laugh out loud, I'm boisterous.
> Laughter causes
> such aggravation, better hold mine in for a while.

456 (2,294)

> Sparrows chattering
> after the sun has set,
> half a branch is enough for your tiny bodies.
> Why then covet
> the mighty forest?

457 (Shim 24)

I despised the crow for being black outside,
unaware that inside it was white.
I loved the seagull for being white outside, unaware that inside it
    was black.
Now I hope
I know outside, inside, black and white.

458 (1,326)

"Ahem, who's there?" comes cough and query.
"It's the nun from the temple opposite."
"Why come to the room of an old widower monk who sleeps alone?"
"I've come
to put my bonnet on the peg where you hang your cap."

459 (1,734)

Is anything more hateful
than the spider?
Unraveling his guts he spins his broad web,
to catch
every butterfly that dances for a flower.

460 (897)

I'll set a hundred plants,
but no more bamboo for me:
the bamboo pipe wails, the bamboo arrow flies, the bamboo brush pines.
Why set bamboo
when all it does is wail, fly, and pine?

461 (644)

"People, kind people, please buy my powder and rouge."
"Vendor, good vendor, I'll buy, if your wares are fine."
"How fine my wares are I cannot say, but once rubbed on, you'll have
    an allure not previously yours."
"If your claims,
vendor, are true, five, six large measures is what I'll buy,
    even if I have to sell my old underwear."

462 (690)

> A toad grabbed a fly in its mouth
> and hopped on a compost pile.
> It looked across at the mountain opposite and saw a peregrine falcon
>     hovering in flight. The toad shuddered, started, tumbled from atop
>     the compost pile.
> Fortunately the toad
> was exceptionally agile, otherwise severe contusions might have been
>     its lot.

463 (22)

> Is the crow black because someone dyed it?
> Is the heron white because someone washed it?
> Are the crane's legs long because someone pulled them out? Are the
>     duck's legs short because someone cut them off?
> Black, white,
> long, short, what's the point in endless wrangling?

464 (1,042)

> I live at the foot of the mountain;
> even the cuckoo embarrasses me.
> It laughs at the size of my cooking pot when it peeks into my house.
> Believe me, bird,
> it's plenty big in terms of my interest in the world.

465 (Shim 169)

> Mountain valleys, words you have none,
> but how could I be ignorant of your disposition?
> All my life benevolence and wisdom have delighted in your company.
> People of the world,
> ask not what I do! I am a man of leisure: I dig herbs; I fish streams.

466 (496)

> "Herdboy, on the long green grassy bank,
> back to front astride the yellow calf,
> are you acquainted with the wrangling of this world?"

The boy
plays his pipe, his only answer a smile.

## Drinking Songs

*Shijo* drinking songs constantly refer to the poet as being drunk, tipsy, and merry. All of these are translations of the character *zui* in Chinese, *ch'ui* in Korean. The idea of being drunk is conventional. It implies that the poet has reached a state wherein he can transcend the cares of a troubled world.

The typical drinking song is convivial. The poet puts away the cares of the world and relaxes in the company of his friends, a temporary but nonetheless healthful expedient.

467 (158)

> Petals fall, new leaves sprout;
> greenness spreads throughout the trees.
> I cut some pine branches, sweep up the catkins,
> and barely attain
> a drunken sleep when an oriole calling a friend awakens me.

468 (167)
Flowers, wine, the moon, and a friend are the four traditional delights of the simple man in nature.

> The flowers have bloomed; the wine is mature;
> the moon is bright; my friend has come.
> This surely calls for something special.
> I'll honor
> these four delights by drinking the long night through.

469 (589)
A reference to Li Bai's delight in both wine and the moon.

> Wine cup in hand I open the window
> to ask a question of the moon.
> The moon is still round, its light still bright, just as it's always been,
> but Li Bai is gone:
> who can understand the message now?

470 (73)

> The donkey is clearly lame;
> don't drive him on the whip.
> When the sun goes down behind west mountain, won't the moon
>     come up in its place?
> On the way
> I may drop into a wine house; who knows when I'll leave?

471 (1,242)

> When my legs give way after drinking wine,
> I swear I'll never touch the stuff again.
> But the oaths I swear count for nothing when next I hold a cup and look
>     at it.
> So be it:
> what's the point in talking about oaths I took when I was drunk?

472 (716)

This poem echoes Li Bai in a number of phrases including the simple joy of
wine and the lengthy drinking session.

> The water of ten thousand blue waves
> failed to wash away my thousand cares;
> yet a single jug of wine has washed them clean today.
> Thus Li Bai
> stayed drunk all the time.

473 (32)

> Autumn rain never amounts to much;
> no need to lay out my raincoat.
> Ten *li* is not very far; no need to drive the lame donkey.
> On the way
> I may drop into a wine house; who knows when I'll leave!

474 (8)

In ancient China Liu Ling was famous for his love of wine.

> Borne flat or upright—
> when I'm dead, will I know?

Plow a dry field above my grave or weed a wet field, it's all the same.
Wine won't find
its way to Liu Ling's grave? Better drink my fill while I may.

475 (2,323)

I thought I was traveling alone,
but the moon has come with me.
Had I known it was coming, I'd have brought some wine along.
So be it:
why not borrow some from the master and get drunk before continuing
   on my way?

476 (601)
"Midsummer" is literally the sixth month in the lunar calendar.

The moon is so bright
the Third Watch is like daylight.
The breeze is so cool midsummer is like autumn.
Breeze fresh,
moon bright, how can I avoid a party mood?

477 (488)

Along a hill, thick with green willows and fragrant grasses,
a boy rides an ox.
A rain-drenched traveler asks where the wine is sold.
"Ask over there
where apricot blossoms flutter in the sky."

478 (1,944)

I'll build a house and roof it with clouds,
dig a well and in it float the moon.
With the spring wind I'll make a broom and sweep up the falling flowers.
My wine
bearing friend, why won't he find me?

479 (435)

When did I ever delight in wine?
I always knew wine was mad medicine.
But the undivided loyal heart, burdened with ten thousand cares and
    troubles,
how can it
endure now without the solace of a cup?

480 (1,946)

Who pierced the paper window?
The moon is in the wine jug.
If I drink this wine, I drink the moonlight with it.
And if I drink
the moonlight, surely the inner me will brighten.

481 (1,251)

Wine, why do you redden
a white face?
Instead of reddening a white face why not blacken white hair?
Should you really
blacken white hair, I'll drink and drink, I'll never sober up again.

## Songs of Nature

In an essay on the Korean approach to nature, Chŏng Pyŏng'uk points out
that Korean poets usually eschew an objective view of nature in favor of an
internalized, conceptualized, subjective view. In other words, nature is an
object of contemplation—contemplation that leads not to rapture over the
physically beautiful but to delight in the morally beautiful.

482 (1,177)

The world has abandoned me;
abandoned thus, I wander around.
Seated sideways on my lame donkey, I pass among green trees and
    fragrant grasses,
so intoxicated
by the setting sun I leave my whip behind.

483 (2,298)

> Sun, don't go;
> let's go together, you and I.
> Whither do you hurry in all that vastness of sky?
> How about waiting
> to see the moon rise over east mountain?

484 (1,057)

> With no calendar in the hills
> how can I tell the seasons?
> When flowers bloom, it's spring; when leaves fall, it's autumn,
> and when children
> look for old clothes, then I know it's winter.

485 (103)

Once again "rivers and lakes" translates *kangho*, a reference to a district in China with three rivers and five lakes, with the secondary meaning of the secluded world of the hermit.

> Autumn comes to rivers and lakes;
> skinny fish fatten.
> I load my nets in a skiff and return to blue waves.
> White gull,
> pretend you haven't seen me: the world may discover where I've been.

486 (1,338)

> "Boy, where do you live?"
> "Me, Sir? By the river."
> "What do you do by the river?" "I fish there for a living."
> "That sounds
> like a fine life; I think I'll join you."

487 (267)

> Deaf and blind
> I've come into the hills.
> With nothing to hear, can there be anything to see?
> My lips
> may be whole, but what can I say?

488 (Shim 79)

The road is long;
my house is over that hill.
The moon lights the narrow path that threads the bamboo grove.
My poor
famished donkey, why push him along?

489 (Shim 80)

Has the dew on the withered leaves
already turned to frost?
Autumn waters are broad and placid; autumn thoughts renew the heart.
Boy,
raise the sail, push off the boat; we'll go and find a friend.

490 (1,866)

Strains of merry piping delight the ear;
quickly I open the bamboo window.
A fine rain is falling on the long dike; the boy is astride the cow's back.
Boy,
spring has come to rivers and lakes; fetch me my fishing pole.

491 (1,873)

I nodded off; I lost my fishing pole.
I danced a set; I lost my rain cape.
White gull, laugh not at an old man's folly.
Ten *li*
of peach blossoms fill me with the joy of spring.

492 (1,955)

I've hung a windbell outside my green window;
beneath the windbell I've hung a screen of peacock feathers.
Every puff of wind is now a delightful tinkle.
Floating
in and out of sleep, it's like listening to distant bells.

493 (1,038)

I built my thatched hut against a rock
here where mountains and waters are fine.
I fish in the moonlight, till in the clouds.

Hardly enough
to live on, but I desire nothing more.

494 (1,142)

Old man fishing,
wine loaded in the bow,
what did you do with life; did you spend it with a fishing pole?
I've never known
envy in my life, but now I envy you.

495 (737)

My horse takes fright;
I grab the reins and look down.
Blue silk mountains are broidered in the water.
Little horse,
no need to shy away; this is what I came to see.

496 (467)

"Where do you live?"
"Over the mountain,
in the green bamboo grove by the great river, there's a house; the
    brushwood gate is closed.
A gull flies
in front; why not go there and ask?"

497 (360)

Fallen leaves kicked by my horse's hooves,
every leaf the voice of autumn.
The god of the winds becomes a broom and sweeps the leaves away.
One moment,
please: why not leave this rough mountain path covered as it is?

498 (21)

Crow after crow;
why do they cry through the night.
Cry after cry, each cry something new.
Boy,
don't tune the *kŏmun'go*; you'll frighten that crow away.

499 (446)

My house is very remote;
the cuckoo calls by day.
Countless valleys and peaks keep my brushwood gate closed.
Even the dog
doesn't bark here; it dozes as white petals fall.

500 (Shim 136)

The flower I saw last year
this year I see again.
Sweet fragrance, how glad I am to see you: are you glad to see me?
Sadly,
the flower makes no reply.

501 (888)

White snow fills all heaven and earth;
a thousand peaks are jade jewels.
The plum is half open; bamboo leaves are green.
Boy,
fill my cup; I feel that special tingle.

502 (586)

Autumn leaves are tinged half red;
the stream is limpid clear.
I cast my net in the fast water and lie down on the rock.
It seems
I am the only man of leisure in this entire world.

503 (Shim 111)

Sunset on the river village;
fishing lanterns everywhere.
Fisherfolk crowd the river; they offer sacrifice to the beat of the drum.
Oars splashing
in the night augment the mountain quiet.

## Songs of Mortality

Human mortality has always been a favorite *shijo* theme. Poems abound with references to fallen petals, autumn leaves, and the passing of the seasons. References to white hair are no less frequent. While mourning the inevitability of human mortality, *shijo* poets manage to accept their fate, in the process revealing a wry sense of humor and a certain dedication to the principles of carpe diem.

504 (2,092)

> Young men in your prime,
> do not mock white-haired old men.
> Under a just heaven will you always be young?
> For us, too,
> the joys of youth are as yesterday.

505 (2,160)

> Spring breezes blow briefly;
> they melt the piled snow.
> The green hills show their old faces again.
> Old frosted locks,
> could they possibly melt?

506 (289)

This is a reference to the ancient legend that there is a golden crow at the center of the sun and a jade rabbit at the center of the moon.

> Golden crow and jade rabbit,
> who is chasing you
> that you skim so rapidly through the broad plains of the sky?
> From now on
> rest every ten *li?* Then travel on.

507 (2,061)

> Snow falling on the green mountain,
> every peak a jade jewel.
> Spring rain will turn that mountain green again.
> Why, then,
> does white hair never turn black?

508 (781)

The first frost of the year turned into wine
and offered a cup to all the mountains.
Yesterday's green leaves this morning are all tinted red.
If only wine
could turn white hair black, I'd offer a cup to my love.

509 (340)

The elixir here is a herb (*pulloch'o*) said to give eternal youth.

When I was young
I delighted in mountain greens.
Perhaps they contained the elixir of life,
for though my hair
is white now, I do not feel old.

510 (478)

Let's play; let's play while we're young;
we can't play when we grow old.
No flower stays red for ten whole days; the moon when full begins
    to wane.
Life can't go back
to boyhood; let's play while we may.

511 (42)

Autumn in this poem is the ninth and tenth lunar months.

Girl, don't be so haughty;
don't boast of your beauty.
Have you never seen the wild chrysanthemums that bloom on the hill
    behind your house?
One touch of
autumn frost and they become kindling for the fire.

512 (154)

Flower, trust not in beauty;
forbid not the butterfly's favor.
Spring sunlight is fleet; even you should know this.
When leaves and fruit
are so thick that every branch is shade, where will the butterflies be?

513 (339)

> To sun and moon
> I voice my complaint:
> What's so urgent in all that vast expanse of sky
> that you make
> this body, averse to neither wine nor women, so old so quick?

514 (512)

> Lie down and I don't want to get up;
> sit down and I don't want to stand.
> Wine I can't drink like I could; sleep doesn't come like it did.
> I'm afraid
> the good things in life are too few to give me pleasure.

515 (539)

> Growing old is a grievous pill;
> I thought it just involved white hair,
> but I'm hard of hearing, my teeth are falling out—white hair is the
>       least of it.
> Need I add:
> the beautiful lady of the night looks at me as she'd look at a bitter
>       cucumber.

516 (1,404)

> Ah, you cheated me,
> autumn moon and spring breeze, you cheated me!
> You always came at your bidden time; I thought you could be trusted,
> but you gave me
> all your white hairs and went chasing after youth.

517 (535)

> This old sick body
> lies in a grass hut.
> A cool breeze opens the door; a shaft of moonlight enters the room.
> Leave them be:
> cool breeze and bright moon are my friends.

518 (1,336)
*Makkŏlli* is unrefined rice wine.

> Ninety-nine years old, that old man
> drinks strained *makkŏlli* till drunk.
> Don't laugh, young rascals, when he pitches, staggers, stumbles, along
>     the broad road home.
> Our hearts, too,
> were young yesterday.

519 (1,322)

> Oh youth,
> where did you go?
> While I immersed myself in wine and women, you changed places with
>     white hair.
> Now, no matter
> how I search, can you come easily again?

520 (Shim 46)

> Just because you're a beauty
> don't tear a man's innards out.
> Can I, like you, grab time on the flood?
> When white hair
> streams under your ears, perhaps you'll know regret.

521 (Shim 47)

> Girl, look at that flower:
> it fell while still full-blown.
> Your face may be jade, but can you put a tether on youth?
> When you grow old
> and the traffic at your door is not what it was of yore, that's when
>     you'll learn regret.

## Love Songs

An enormous number of anonymous poems deal with love-related themes.
Scholars say this is as a direct result of the cloak, and consequent freedom,
provided by anonymity. Some of the anonymous love songs are at variance
with Confucian values; a few are even quite gross. The majority, however,

mine such a vein of rich humor that they delight the modern reader. In the
traditional love *shijo*, the lovers never meet. The poet is usually content to re-
count the feelings of one or other of the parties. The anonymous *shijo*, how-
ever, does not hesitate to bring the lovers together and the resultant dra-
matic tension gives the poems an added dimension. The love poems are so
numerous that some sort of division seemed warranted. Hence, the poems
have here been divided into Love Songs and Songs of Parting. The division
is arbitrary and only for convenience' sake.

522 (1,244)

> Iced rice water
> when merry with wine;
> taking my lover in my arms again when he's about to leave at dawn.
> What if others
> discover these two great pleasures in life?

523 (334)

The butterfly and swallowtail (a butterfly with tiger-like markings) symbol-
ize the male, and flower and leaf the female. The poem is also interpreted as
the expression of a desire to quit the turbulent world of men and to retire,
even for a brief respite, to the simple joys of nature.

> Butterfly, let's go to the green mountain;
> swallowtail, you come, too.
> If darkness catches us on the road, let's spend the night on a flower.
> If the flower
> should prove inhospitable, we can always sleep on a leaf.

524 (738)

One commentator notes that wine-spring (*jiuquan*) refers to a legendary
place in China where springwater tasted like wine. Others say that it is sim-
ply the name of a wine house.

> Ride a horse through a field of flowers
> and the scent lingers on the hoof.
> Enter a wine-spring tavern and the smell of undrunk wine sticks fast.
> All we did
> was catch each other's eye; why then all the lies?

525 (120)
This poem probably refers to rivalry between wife and concubine.

> Beckoned to the house opposite,
> ordered into my own.
> Should I go in and close the door, or should I go to that beckoning hand?
> I'll become
> two bodies; then I can be here and go there.

526 (1,023)

> What is love like?
> It is round or is it square?
> Is it long or is it short? Can you pace it, can you measure it?
> The length of love
> I do not know, but it's long enough to tear your innards out.

527 (1,423)

> Last night I slept alone, curled like a shrimp,
> and the night before I slept alone, curled like a shrimp.
> Is this any life for a man, to sleep long days and nights curled like
>     a shrimp?
> But today
> my love has come, and tonight I look forward to stretched legs and
>     relaxed sleep.

528 (169)

> Are fallen flowers all beautiful?
> A flower without fragrance is no flower at all.
> Are friends all truly friends? A friend without affection is no friend at all.
> It seems to me
> that only my love is truly fragrant, truly affectionate.

529 (427)

> Don't give my love to another;
> don't crave another's love.
> For frivolous love may mingle with our pure love.
> With a lifetime
> of love, we'll enjoy a hundred years together.

530 (53)

The magpie is traditionally a bearer of good news.

> My dreams were sweet last night
> and the magpie cried at dawn.
> Signs, perhaps, that I was going to see you.
> My love,
> you're here at last; why not sleep before you leave?

531 (602)

This poem possibly echoes Li Bai's *Jiang jin jiu* in which the poet exchanges horse and furs for wine. Here the plea is for time rather than wine. The cock as a traditional symbol of punctuality or regularity increases the whimsical humor.

> Cock, don't crow. I'll take off my clothes
> and give you what the pawnshop gives.
> Day, don't dawn, I entreat the cock,
> but the insensible
> east gets brighter and brighter.

532 (597)

> Moon, round moon, moon that shines
> through my beloved's east window,
> does he lie alone, or does he hold some young love in his arms?
> Moon,
> tell it as you see it; for me this is life and death.

533 (1,020)

> One by one I've gathered up my feelings of love;
> I've measured them, bagged them.
> They're loaded now on the straight back of a fine strong horse.
> Hey, lad,
> give her the whip; send them off to my love.

534 (45)

> When I grasp my girl's wrist,
> how coyly she smiles.
> When I reach across her shoulder to scratch her back, she creeps closer
>     and puts her arms around me.
> Love,
> don't come too close; I cannot bear it.

535 (1,173)

> In this world medicine is plentiful
> and sharp knives abound, they say,
> but there's no knife to cut off affection, no medicine to forget true love.
> So be it:
> I'll leave my cutting and forgetting till I go to the other world.

536 (1,180)

> Holding up the hem of her purple mantle
> as she moves in the fine rain,
> a girl hurries toward pear blossom valley.
> Captivated
> by someone's lies, she's unaware of getting wet.

537 (1,016)

> Feelings of love fuse into fire;
> it burns within my heart.
> Insides perish and fuse into water; it spurts from my two eyes.
> One body,
> invaded by water and fire, I wonder will I live or die?

538 (579)

> My love is coming! I take dinner early, run out the middle gate, to the
>     outside gate and sit on the step. I shield my eyes with my hand. Is he
>     coming or not?
> I look at the mountain opposite. Something black and white is standing
>     there: it must be my love.

Stockings clutched to my breast, shoes in my hand, I begin to run,
    racing, rolling, faster, still faster, oblivious of dry ground or wet—
    for I have words of love to say. One quick look tells me all: last
    year's stripped flax stalks have deceived me.
Luckily,
it is night, for if it were day, I'd be the laughingstock of the place.

## 539 (1,958)

Something flickered outside the window;
I thought it was my love.
I sprang to my feet and went outside. It was not my love. Clouds
    streaming past a dim moon had deceived me.
Luckily,
it was night, for if it were day, I'd be the laughingstock of the place.

## 540 (1,280)

The dog barks at the brushwood gate:
thinking only of my love, I go out to see.
It is not my love. The bright moon fills the yard. The sound I heard was
    leaves falling in a puff of autumn wind.
Dog,
why do you deceive me, barking pointlessly at leaves falling in the
    autumn wind?

## 541 (980)

The dog and cock are symbols of faithfulness and punctuality, respectively.

Of flying birds and beasts that crawl,
cock and dog are marked out for a fall.
For when within the green gauze screen my love lies sleeping on my
    breast, the cock cries loud and raucous and routs him from his rest.
    And when he comes to the outer gate, the dog makes such a snapping,
    barking flurry that my love must take his leave, departing in a hurry.
Poultry-peddlers,
dog-meat-mongers, when next you cry outside my gate, you'll get that
    cock and dog trussed tightly for the plate.

542 (106)
Chŏng Pyŏng'uk's *Munhak sajŏn* notes that the word translated here as
"food" is unknown.

> Dog, black dog, fool of a dog
> with long droopy ears,
> the food I was going to eat myself I'm giving now to you.
> So when my love
> comes in the night, for goodness sake, stay quiet.

543 (605)

> At the first crow of the cock
> don't get up and leave.
> Sit there a while till the cock crows again.
> That cock
> is from another place: he's crying for his mother.

544 (1,100)
A satirical treatment of marriage in the racy manner of the *sasŏl shijo* of the
eighteenth century. The translation takes some liberties, especially in the
second section where the imagery is expressed in terms of native place,
Chŏlla and Hamgyŏng Province, rather than vessel.

> Six crock bowls the bride smashed
> in a fit of temper on her wedding night.
> "Are you going to replace them?" mother-in-law asked. The bride
>  replied: "Your son has smashed beyond repair the vessel I
>  brought from home.
> One weighed
> against the other, the balance would seem quite fair."

545 (4)

> Change your mind and come back if you wish,
> but on the way you mustn't change your mind again.
> Hate may change to love, but love must not change to hate.
> Hate or love,
> whichever it may be, I'm going to sleep here tonight.

546 (44)

Girl, I hear you have a field of early rice,
well-watered and fertile too.
Should you consider taking a tenant, I'm the man, I have the tools.
Should you give
your field to me, I'll take my plow and scatter the seed.

547 (1,610)

We fixed our tryst for the rising of the moon:
the cock has crowed, but still he hasn't come.
Has he met a new love, has an old flame waylaid him?
Our relationship
may have been fleeting, but how could he deceive me so?

548 (880)

White-haired, but wanton still,
she eyed a bright young spark.
Hair dyed black, she panted to the mountain top, but as she crested the
    topmost ridge a sudden burst of rain stained her white collar black
    and turned her black hair white again.
Thus the matron's
hopes were raised and shattered in a trice.

549 (76)

Why do insects cry in the grass
when the moon is so bright at night?
If my lover cannot come, could he not at least send me sleep?
Waiting now
for sleep to come, a greater sorrow fills my heart.

550 (153)

Look at the butterfly, how it dances for the flower,
and the flower, how it smiles with undisguised delight
in joyful renewal of their seasonal love affair.
Why is it
that human love once gone never comes back again?

551 (1,664)

A reference to the ancient legend of Emperor Wang of Shu who fell in love with the wife of one of his ministers and was metamorphosed into a cuckoo.

> When I'm dead and gone,
> the spirit of a cuckoo I'll become.
> I'll hide in the branches of a flowering pear tree,
> and cry
> so sadly at night my love will surely hear me.

552 (1,009)

> Where is a man sent
> when he dies?
> In the next world as in this, is he sent to his love?
> Were this really so,
> I'd die and go there now.

553 (281)

Another reference to Emperor Wang of Shu, who became a cuckoo after death.

> What's the point in longing?
> Soon I'll be dead,
> and become the spirit of a cuckoo; I'll perch on the branches of a pear tree,
> and I'll keep on crying
> outside the blue silk window of my beloved.

554 (513)

> Will sleep come if I lie down,
> will my love come if I wait?
> Though I lie down, how can I hope to sleep?
> Better spend
> the long night where I sit.

555 (58)

The magpie traditionally is associated with the bringing of good news.

> My dreams were sweet last night
> and the magpie chattered this morning.

Fair signs, I believe, that I will see my love.
I'm glad,
so glad: words cannot tell my joy.

556 (2,280)

A tear on the first letter,
a sigh on the second,
letters and lines an India ink landscape.
My love,
you've written to me in tears; I think I should forgive you.

557 (19)

Does paint make the crow black?
Does age make the heron white?
Some things are black and some are white; it's their nature from of old.
How, then,
can my love say, black and white, I am both?

558 (2,275)

My sighs will be the breeze,
my tears a fine rain,
to blow on the windows and splatter the panes of the room where my
     beloved sleeps,
thus to waken him
from a deep sleep of forgetfulness.

559 (578)

My love said he'd come,
but the moon has set and the morning star has risen.
Does the fault lie with him who deceives or with me for waiting?
From now on,
can I believe him, even if he insists he's coming?

560 (1,575)

If, born again in the next life,
you became me and I you,
and your heart was torn with the love I feel for you,
then perhaps
you'd discover the sorrow I bear in this world.

561 (1,593)

> With tears I beg you: don't brush aside
> the hand that clutches your sleeve.
> You are a man; if you go you will forget.
> I'm your mistress,
> a woman: I can never forget.

562 (433)

> Could I be ignorant
> of my own lack of beauty?
> No rouge adorns my face; powder I never use.
> Looking as I do,
> how could I ask anyone to love me?

563 (249)

> Dream, silly dream,
> have you sent my love away?
> Better you had woken me up than send my love away.
> From now on,
> if my love comes, hold him fast and wake me up.

564 (5)

> My love has gone; forgotten me, it seems;
> he doesn't appear even in my dreams.
> Surely, love, you couldn't forget in such a brief time?
> So narrow-minded
> am I now, I blame everything on him.

565 (40)

> Girls, buy all the heat you can,
> early heat, late heat, heat that's been a year around.
> If buy you will, girls, buy all that's in your heart of summer dog days' heat
>     when you meet your love on a moonswept sleeping bench, encoiled
>     whereon you do whatever makes innards boil, sweat beads rise, and
>     breath come rasping harsh. And buy that heat from long midwinter
>     nights, when your love and you are joined beneath the covers in the
>     lower corner, and hands and feet grow fidgety, and throat begins

to burn until you're driven to gulp large measures of iced rice water
stored in the upper corner.
Heat vendor,
of all your many heats on sale, who could be averse to this loving pair?
Sell them not to others: sell them just to me.

566 (48)

Woman, your face once beautiful is like that red willow tree
across the stream that stood so lone and straight and now is but a
rotten, wrinkled stump!
Youth, ah youth! If only you were three by five,
if only
you were fifteen years younger, with you I'd have my way.

567 (50)

Girl, I've painted a plum tree
in India ink on your green silk dress.
I've painted it without roots, branches, or leaves,
lest when the
flowering season comes your thoughts should be with another.

568 (88)

Traveling through the winter scape
of Kangwŏn's Diamond Mountains,
I saw a white falcon perched on the tip of the fir tree that stands tall
behind Yuchŏm-sa Temple. I caught it, tamed it, and sent it to
hunt pheasants.
Sad to say,
my new found love I can neither catch nor tame.

569 (310)

You beg a man like me who wouldn't eat honey cakes
fried in oil to eat stone-filled *mandu* dumplings boiled in cold water.
You beg a man like me who wouldn't consort with P'yŏngyang *kisaeng*
to give in to your desire.
Beg you may,
my girl, but nothing could make me take you in my arms.

570 (321)
Mengchangjun (Maengsanggun in Korean) lived during the Warring States period (403–221 B.C.) in China. As prime minister, he was distinguished by generosity and an extraordinary regard for the coat of the silver fox. Samgaksan is a mountain in North P'yŏngan Province, North Korea.

When I think of you, my love,
I think of you as Mengchangjun's fox fur coat.
But when you think of me, my love, you think of me as the gapped comb
    of an old toothless monk in Chunghŭng Temple, Samgaksan.
Heaven knows
the pleasure of unrequited love; pass this pleasure, please, around.

571 (667)

It is the third watch. The girl in the bridal bedroom is so gentle,
so beautiful, I look and look again; I can't believe my eyes.
Sixteen years old, peach blossom complexion, golden hairpin, white
    ramie skirt, bright eyes agleam in playful glance, lips half-parted
    in a smile. My love! My own true love!
Need I say aught
of the silver in her voice and the wonder of her under the quilt.

572 (825)

Winds rest before crossing that ridge,
even clouds rest before the crossing.
Wild falcons, hand-reared falcons, peregrine falcons, yearling falcons
    all rest before crossing the topmost peak of Changsŏng Mountain
    Pass.
But were my love
on the other side, I'd cross that ridge without a single pause.

573 (1,396)

Ah, I saw him;
I saw my monk supreme.
Such beauty wrapped in an old ragged robe!
A camellia
flowered in midwinter's snow and crept into an old pine tree.

574 (1,410)

Love, why don't you come!
Why don't you come!
On the way did someone build a castle of iron, erect a wall within the
    castle, build a house within the wall, place a rice-chest within the
    house, put a box within the rice-chest, tie you up within the box,
    make the box fast with a pair of dragon-turtle locks? Why don't
    you come?
With thirty days
in the month, surely you could save one day for me?

575 (1,574)

My thundering love I meet
like a lightning flash.
Like rain our coming together; like clouds our breaking apart.
Sighs gush
from deep inside: swirling mists in flower.

576 (1,793)

Rip your black robe asunder; fashion a pair of breeches.
Take off your rosary; use it for the donkey's crupper.
These ten years studying Buddha's Pure Land, invoking the Goddess of
    Mercy and Amitabha's saving hand, let them go where they will.
Night on a nun's breast
is no time for reciting sutras.

577 (1,914)

The monk that slept here must, after all, have been a man.
How I miss him, now he's gone!
I pillowed my head on his pine winter hat and he pillowed his on my
    festive headpiece. With his long robe I covered myself and he covered
    himself with my skirt. In the night I awoke to truth: our love filled
    hat and headpiece.
Pondering
all next day, my heart was quite undone.

578 (Shim 73)

The wind that blew open the brushwood gate last night
deceived me completely.
The paper window rattled. My love, I thought, with joy, but I was wrong.
Had word gone
abroad, night itself would have laughed me to scorn.

579 (553)

I wanted to forget;
the more I tried the more in love I became.
I took sick; everyone laughed.
One thing leads
to another; I grow sadder every day.

580 (Shim 196)

Fair as a flower,
my love ripens into fruit.
Can my soul forget the love that stretches across the branches?
What if you
become a fallen leaf, victim of a crazy wind?

581 (Shim 70)

On the evidence of last night's encounter
who can say
whether it was the jabbering of a parrot or the deceitful call of a cuckoo?
I wonder
if the powder on my cheek left its mark?

582 (1,597)

Your teeth gleam when you smile;
lovelier still the glint of anger in your eye.
Sit, stand, walk, run: let's see the range of your girlish allure. Ha, ha,
    you, my girl, are going to be mine!
Your parents
brought you into the world so that you might love only me.

583 (1,149)

> A snow moon fills the window:
> wind, don't blow.
> I know full well it's not the sound of gliding slippers,
> but when lonely
> and filled with longing, I wonder is it she?

## Songs of Parting

584 (330)

> Like a hen-pheasant chased by a hawk,
> without tree, rock, or stone for cover—
> Like a sailor on the high seas, a thousand bags of grain aboard, oars lost,
>     sails lost, rigging torn, mast broken, rudder gone, wind blowing, waves
>     breaking, shrouded in fog, day fading fast, ten thousand *li* to go,
>     darkness falling all around, the world a foaming, seething wave, and
>     now suddenly beset by pirates!
> Can this compare
> with how I felt parting from my love two days ago?

585 (359)

> I'll draw two characters on a fallen leaf
> and fly it high in the north-west wind.
> I'll send it to my love in the bright moonlit capital.
> How sad
> he'll truly be when he reads it.

586 (735)

> My horse is neighing for the road,
> but my love won't let me go.
> The sun is crossing the mountain and I've a thousand *li* to go.
> Don't stop me,
> love, stop the setting sun.

587 (600)

> They say the moon can see my beloved;
> I wish I could see that moon.
> I half open my east window and wait for the moon to rise.
> Tears flow
> like rain; the moon is shadowed as well.

588 (573)

> I drew a picture of my love
> and placed it beside my pillow.
> Sitting, standing, I touch it fondly and say:
> love, speak to me,
> I do not know where to put my heart.

589 (165)

Falling petals are a traditional symbol of transience; the cuckoo is a symbol of unhappy love.

> Flowers may fall or no;
> cuckoos may sing or no,
> but should I meet again my love from days of old,
> could falling petals
> or singing birds make me sad?

590 (1,021)

> I want to buy love,
> but who will sell it;
> I want to sell parting, but who will buy it.
> With no one
> to sell love or buy parting, I'm afraid eternal love means eternal parting.

591 (49)

> Parting turns to fire.
> Oh, how my innards burn!
> You'd think that tears become rain would quench that blaze,
> but sighs
> become the wind keep fanning the flames.

592 (1,680)

> Parting turns to fire;
> it burns my innards up.
> Tears become rain; perhaps they'll quench that fire.
> But sighs
> become the wind; will the fire live or die?

593 (80)

Wild geese and carp symbolize communication between parted loved ones.

> You men with guns on the riverbank,
> shoot all the wild geese!
> You men with fishing nets, catch all the carp!
> For neither
> wild geese nor carp bring any news.

594 (306)

> I'll catch the wild goose,
> befriend him, tame him.
> I'll teach him well the road to where my true love dwells.
> At night,
> when thoughts of my love rise in my mind, the wild goose can take
> a message.

595 (305)

> The wild geese have flown away;
> who will bring me news?
> I try to dream, but one must sleep to dream.
> My love stole
> sleep when he left. What's the use of further thought?

596 (2,086)

> Wild goose, soaring in the blue,
> when you pass my true love's house,
> if you can't deliver a letter, at least give him a message.
> Tell him:
> the moon is bright, the night interminable and I miss him.

597 (592)
The wild goose also is associated with deep, enduring love.

> Bright moon, chill wind,
> long night, no sleep.
> Wild goose, crying as you fly north,
> in mourning
> a lost mate, are you and I any different?

598 (979)

> I wonder a moment
> why this fan was sent to me.
> It was sent to quench the flame in my heart.
> But how can a fan
> quench a flame that even tears cannot quench?

599 (2,212)

> Letter, do you come alone;
> where is your master?
> Are you the only traveler on the broad streets of the capital?
> From now on,
> I don't want you, I want your master.

600 (417)
The *haegŭm* is a two-stringed fiddle. The bird is variously identified as a Siberian peregrine falcon or a duck hawk.

> The love that lights my eyes
> is not very far away.
> Should I sing a song; should I strum the *haegŭm?*
> No, I'll change
> into a hawk and snatch her to my side.

601 (1,765)

> I awoke from sleep
> to find a letter from my love.
> I unfolded it a hundred times and placed it on my breast.
> The letter
> was not very heavy, but my heart was weighted down.

602 (7)

Ring, you've lost your mate;
you're all alone with me.
When you find your mate, I'll see my love again.
When it comes
to regret for a lost mate, is there any difference between you and me?

603 (2)

I'm going now, but meet again we must,
or how will I survive my longing to see you.
Even a thousand *li* apart, won't I see you in my dreams?
But when I wake
and you are not beside me, what will I do?

604 (1,537)

On the way to see my love,
mountains seem like hills.
But when at last my leave I must take, the hills seem like high mountains.
Better
if those hills were so high I couldn't cross them.

605 (117)

That face reflected in the mirror
to me is like a flower.
How much the more when all made up I show myself to my love.
How sad to think
I cannot show myself thus to him.

606 (2,273)

Sigh, why do you come to me
as soon as the sun goes down?
Night after night you keep me awake; you are my enemy.
Parting
is a commonplace of human life; why not spread your custom around?

607 (320)

> I'm leaving now;
> my love I leave behind.
> But if I do, you must love my love as you would love me.
> Love,
> if you are treated coldly, go where you can find love.

608 (575)

> When my love and I parted
> he caught my sleeve and said:
> I'll return before the cherry blossoms bloom outside your window.
> The blossoms
> have fallen, new leaves have sprouted, and still I have no news.

609 (29)

> With my sharp knife I cut a length of light
> from a rain-cleared autumn sky;
> I made a suit and broidered it, using a fine silver needle and five-
>     colored thread.
> Why? To send
> it to my love who lives in the palace.

610 (2,082)

> Lone wild goose, crying as you fly;
> fly no more, listen to my sighs.
> Drop into Hanyang Fortress and bring my love this message. Tell
>     him I sit alone, abandoned in the women's quarters, oppressed,
>     depressed by the yellow waning moon. I cannot endure, tell him,
>     because I miss him so.
> Friend, we, too,
> are in a rush for love; I'm not sure I can pass your message on.

611 (609)

> The anchor is raised; the boat sails away;
> when will it return?
> Across the broad seas it voyages; come back, come back soon.
> The rhythmic chant
> of oarsmen in the night cuts my heart to shreds.

*Reference Matter*

# Chronology of the Chosŏn Dynasty Kings

| | |
|---|---|
| T'aejo | 1392–98 |
| Chŏngjong | 1398–1400 |
| T'aejong | 1400–1418 |
| Sejong | 1418–50 |
| Munjong | 1450–52 |
| Tanjong | 1452–55 |
| Sejo | 1455–68 |
| Yejong | 1468–69 |
| Sŏngjong | 1469–94 |
| Yŏnsan'gun | 1494–1506 |
| Chungjong | 1506–44 |
| Injong | 1544–45 |
| Myŏngjong | 1545–67 |
| Sŏnjo | 1567–1608 |
| Kwanghaegun | 1608–23 |
| Injo | 1623–49 |
| Hyojong | 1649–59 |
| Hyŏnjong | 1659–74 |
| Sukjong | 1674–1720 |

| Kyŏngjong | 1720–24 |
| Yŏngjo | 1724–76 |
| Chŏngjo | 1776–1800 |
| Sunjo | 1800–1834 |
| Hŏnjong | 1834–49 |
| Ch'ŏljong | 1849–63 |
| Kojong | 1863–1907 |
| Sunjong | 1907–10 |

# Bibliography

An Chasan. *Chosŏn munhhaksa* (History of Chosŏn literature). Seoul: Hanilsŏjŏn, 1922.

———. *Shijo shihak* (The poetics of *shijo*). Seoul: Kyomunsa, 1949.

Cho Kyuik. *Kagokch'angsaŭi kungmunhakchŏk ponjil* (The essence of the *kagok-ch'ang* song lyric in the Korean literary tradition). Seoul: Chimmundang, 1994.

Cho Tongil. *Han'guk munhak t'ongsa* (Comprehensive history of Korean literature). Seoul: Chishik sanŏpsa, 1989.

Cho Yunche. *Chosŏn shigaŭi yŏn'gu* (A study of Chosŏn poetry). Seoul: Chisŏmunhwasa, 1948.

Ch'oe Tongwŏn. *Koshijo non'go* (Studies in classical *shijo*). Seoul: Samyŏngsa, 1990.

Chŏn Kyut'ae. *Han'guk shiga yŏn'gu* (Studies in Korean poetry). Seoul: Koryŏwŏn, 1986.

Chŏng Chaeho; Kungmunhakhoe, ed. *Ch'ŏnggu yŏng'ŏn p'yŏnch'an ŭishik ko* (*Ch'ŏnggu yŏng'ŏn*: a study of editorial awareness). Seoul: T'aehaksa, 1997.

Chŏng Pyŏng'uk. *Han'guk kojŏn shigaron* (A study of classical Korean poetry). Seoul: Shin'gu munhwasa, 1988.

———. *Han'guk shigaŭi unyulgwa hyŏngt'ae* (Rhythm and form in Korean poetry). Seoul: Semunsa, 1984.

———. *Shijo munhak sajŏn* (Dictionary of *shijo* literature). Seoul: Shin'gu munwhasa, 1974.

Kim Chehyŏn. *Shijo munhangnon* (A study of *shijo* literature). Seoul: Yejŏnsa, 1975.

Kim Chinu. "Shijoŭi unyul kujoŭi saegoch'al" (A new study of the structure of *shijo* rhythm). '*Han'gŭl' 60 tol kinyŏm t'ŭkchip* 1 (1981).

Kim Sangsŏn. *Han'guk shiga hyŏngt'aeron* (A study of form in Korean poetry). Seoul: Ilchogak, 1979.

Kim Taehaeng. *Shijo yuhyŏngnon* (Studies of form in *shijo*). Seoul: Ewha University Press, 1986.

Kwŏn Tuhwan. "Shijoŭi palsaenggwa kiwŏn" (Emergence and origin of *shijo*). In Kungmunhakhoe, ed., *Koshijo yŏn'gu* (Classical *shijo* studies). Seoul: T'aehaksa, 1997.

Lee, Peter. *Korean Literature—Topics and Themes.* Tucson: University of Arizona Press, 1965.

Lee T'aegŭk. *Shijo yŏn'gu nonch'ong* (Compendium of *shijo* studies). Seoul: Ŭlso munhwasa, 1950.

O'Rourke, Kevin. *The Sijo Tradition.* Seoul: Jŏngeumsa, 1987.

Paek Ch'ŏl. *Paek Ch'ŏl munhak chŏnjip* (Paek Ch'ŏl literary miscellany). Seoul: Shin'gu munhwasa, 1968.

Pak Ŭlsu. *Hanguk shijo taesajŏn* (Comprehensive dictionary of Korean *shijo*). Seoul: Asea munhwasa, 1992.

Rutt, Richard. *The Bamboo Grove.* Berkeley: University of California Press, 1971.

Shim Chaewan. *Shijoŭi munhonjŏk yŏ'ngu* (Study of *shijo* records). Seoul: Sejong munhwasa, 1972.

———. *Yŏkdae shijo chŏnso* (Compendium of *shijo* through the ages). Seoul: Sejong munhwasa, 1972.

Yi Pyŏnggi. "Shijoran muŏshin'ga" (What is *shijo*). *Tonga ilbo*, Dec. 10–11, 1926.

———. *Shijoŭi palsaenggwa kagokkwaŭi kubun* (The development of *shijo* and the distinction from *kagok*). Vol. 1. Seoul: Chindanhakbu, 1934.

———. "Shijo wŏllyuron" (A study of the original form of *shijo*). *Shinsaeng*, no. 4 (1929).

# Index of Poets

An Chŏng, 51
An Minyŏng, 145–48
An Sŏu, 116
An Yŏnbo, 152

Chang Man, 86–87
Chin'ok, 155
Cho Chonsŏng, 79
Cho Chun, 37
Cho Hŏn, 76
Cho Hwang, 150–51
Cho Myŏngni, 137
Cho Shik, 54–55
Ch'oe Chikt'ae, 151
Ch'oe Ch'ung, 27
Ch'oe Yŏng, 29
Chŏng Ch'ŏl, 65–75
Chŏng Hŭiryang, 48
Chŏng Mongju, 31–32
Chŏng Mongju's mother, 32
Chŏng On, 87–88
Chŏng T'aehwa, 112–13
Chŏng Tojŏn, 33
Chŏng Tugyŏng, 112
Ch'ŏn'gŭm, 154
Chu Ŭishik, 116

Ha Sunil, 153
Ha Wiji, 40
Han Ho, 76

Hanu, 78
Ho Sŏkkyun, 152
Hong Ikhan, 90
Hong Nang, 112
Hongjang, 155
Hwang Chini, 55–56
Hwang Hŭi, 39–40
Hwang Yunsŏk, 137–38
Hyojong, 113

Im Che, 77–78

Kang Ik, 59–60
Kang Pokchung, 83–84
Kil Chae, 38
Kim Ch'ang'ŏp, 115–16
Kim Changsaeng, 77
Kim Chint'ae, 142
Kim Ch'iu, 153
Kim Chongsŏ, 41
Kim Ch'ŏnt'aek, 117–19
Kim Hag'yŏn, 153
Kim Inhu, 56–57
Kim Koengp'il, 45
Kim Ku, 48–49
Kim Kwang'uk, 88–89
Kim Samhyŏn, 140
Kim Sang'yŏng, 80–81
Kim Sŏngch'oe, 145
Kim Sŏnggi, 143

Kim Sŏng'wŏn, 60
Kim Sujang, 120–31
Kim Tŏngnyŏng, 87
Kim Ugyu, 132
Kim Yŏng, 144
Kim Yugi, 145
Kim Yuk, 89
Kwŏn Homun, 60–62
Kwŏn Ingnyung, 154

Maehwa, 154
Maeng Sasŏng, 38–39

Na Chisŏng, 151
Nam Kuman, 114

Pak Hyogwan, 139–40
Pak Inno, 81–83
Pak P'aengnyŏn, 42
Pak T'aebo, 115
Prince Inp'yŏng, 113–14
Prince Nang'wŏn, 114
Prince Wŏlsan, 46
Prince Yuch'ŏn, 115

Shin Hŏnjo, 138
Shin Hŭm, 84–86
Shin Wi, 138
Sŏ Ik, 75
Sŏ Kyŏngdŏk, 49–50
Song In, 57–58
Song Sun, 50–51
Song T'a, 79
Song Un, 51
Sŏng Hon, 63
Sŏng Sammun, 43
Songgyeyŏnwŏl, 141
Sŏnjo, 78–79

T'aejong, *see* Yi Pang'wŏn
Tanjong, 44–45

U T'ak, 28

Wang Pang'yŏn, 45
Wŏn Ch'ŏnsŏk, 40–41
Wŏn Ho, 46

Yang Saŏn, 58
Yang Ŭngjŏng, 58–59
Yi Chae, 137
Yi Chaemyŏn, 150
Yi Chik, 30
Yi Chŏngbo, 132–36
Yi Chŏngjin, 144–45
Yi Chono, 32–33
Yi Cho'nyŏn, 29
Yi Chungjip, 151
Yi Hubaek, 59
Yi Hwang, 51–54
Yi Hyŏnbo, 46–48
Yi I, 63–65
Yi Kae, 41–42
Yi Kyubo, 28
Yi Myŏnghan, 111
Yi P'ansŏ In'ŭng, 152
Yi Pang'wŏn (T'aejong), 31
Yi Saek, 30
Yi Sebo, 148–50
Yi Sunshin, 77
Yi Tŏg'il, 80
Yi Tŏkhyŏng, 80
Yi Yang'wŏn, 62
Yi Yŏng, 113
Yu Chashin, 62–63
Yu Hŭich'un, 57
Yu Sŏng'wŏn, 44
Yu Ŭngbu, 43–44
Yun Sŏndo, 90–107
Yun Sun, 119
Yun Tusŏ, 117

# Index of First Lines

The numbers in parentheses indicate the numbers used in the collections in which the original, Korean-language texts of the poems are found (see Texts and Sources, pp. 23–24).

A blind man carried (1,188), 162

A blind man on a purblind horse (1,189), 135

A boatman frightened by stormy seas (2,231), 87

A concubine with wine, but who won't give me any (1,240), 160

A crow in sleet appears white (17), 42

A fire blazes in my heart (2,366), 115

A fire starts in the heart (Pak 4,717), 149

A good walker should not run (1,775), 117

A man turns aside from the road (51), 74

A mud-encrusted piece of jade (1,527), 117

A night of wind and snow (Shim 3,113), 79

A pear blossom trembles in a crazy wind (210), 136

A plum branch lay (1,520), 59

A plum petal falls in the spring breeze (2,158), 163

A shadow is reflected in the water (811), 70

A Shilla pagoda, eight hundred years old (1,295), 73

A snow moon fills the window (1,149), 193

A sudden shower (1,223), 66

A tear on the first letter (2,280), 187

A toad grabbed a fly in its mouth (690), 166

A toad, blind in one eye (2,257), 161

After a ten-year interval I see again (1,911), 72

After eating my fill (924), 91

After leaving the world (1,278), 86

After the sun goes down (1,129), 92

Ah, I saw him (1,396), 190

Ah! the day comes to a close (1,398), 107

Ah, the variety (72), 130

Ah, they're cutting it down (1,393), 57

Ah, what have I done? (1,427), 55

Ah, you cheated me (1,404), 177

"Ahem, who's there?" comes cough and query (1,326), 165

All my life I regret (1,735), 27

All my life I've wished (2,216), 135

Along a hill, thick with green willows and fragrant grasses (488), 169

An east wind springs up (679), 96

Are fallen flowers all beautiful? (169), 180

Are heaven and earth different? (119), 103

Are line and pole in proper order (1,887), 104

Are there limits to man's desire for fame and honor? (188), 47

Are you asleep or are you just resting (2,087), 78

As I move the goosefoot forward (113), 71

As I ride along on my lame donkey (1,863), 51

At the end of the day (370), 61

At the first crow of the cock (605), 184

Autumn comes to rivers and lakes (95), 39

Autumn comes to rivers and lakes (103), 171

Autumn comes to the river village (1,226), 101

Autumn leaves are tinged half red (586), 174

Autumn mountains autumn tinted (2,139), 115

Autumn mountains tinted in the fading light (2,138), 62

Autumn night falls on the river (2,136), 46

Autumn rain never amounts to much (32), 168

Bamboo stick, the sight of you (620), 89

Because gold is found in fair waters (287), 42

Beckoned to the house opposite (120), 180

Between heaven and earth (632), 163

Between the twentieth day and the end of the month (2,120), 123

Big brother, little brother (2,313), 73

Birds, don't be sad (156), 160

Black they say is white (122), 127

Blue-cloud skies, yellow-blossom earth (914), 153

Blue mountains go their way (2,055), 57

Blue Stream, do not boast (2,056), 56

Borne flat or upright (8), 168

Boy, don't drive the crows (Shim 1,709), 138

Boy, get ready my rain gear and bamboo hat (1,331), 79

Boy, where do you live? (1,338), 171

Breeze ever fresh (834), 61

Bright moon, chill wind (592), 196

Butterflies hover in pairs where flower blossoms are thick (2,340), 67

Butterfly, let's go to the green mountain (334), 179

Can an old man (1,001), 133

Can medicine cure a sickness (562), 134

Candle, burning within the room (865), 42

Change your mind and come back if you wish (4), 184

Chestnuts are falling (636), 39

Clad in rain hat and straw rain gear (1,082), 45

Clear autumn weather (2,091), 121

Clouds cluster thick (890), 30

Cock, don't crow. I'll take off my clothes (602), 181

Confucius came into this world (193), 125

Could I be ignorant (433), 188

Crane, flying high (2,081), 73

Crossbeams long or short (2,310), 86

Crow after crow (21), 173

Crows fly off to roost (1,766), 105

Cuckoo, crying on the bare mountain (198), 140

Deaf and blind (267), 171

Death may be a bitter pill (1,904), 145

Deep in a valley of Nine Crane Mountain (Shim 308), 150

Desultory rain falls on the paulownia tree (1,495), 48

Did the wind that blew two days ago (1,455), 44

Diverting oneself on rivers and lakes (94), 61

Do not envy the joy of fish (98), 135

Do not exult over fame (183), 140

Does dawn light the east window? (677), 114

Does paint make the crow black? (19), 187

Dog, black dog, fool of a dog (106), 184

Don't bring out the straw mat (1,942), 76

Don't give my love to another (427), 180

Don't go into the water first (2,369), 48

Don't laugh at an old pine (516), 29

Don't mock a gnarled pine (833), 114

Don't talk about others (739), 164

Dragon-like spreading pine (1,565), 142

Dream, silly dream (249), 188

Dream, you brought my love from afar (260), 144

Dressed in hemp through the worst of winter (1,450), 55

Drifting clouds to vent their spleen (468), 60

Drink or can't drink (755), 129

Drink till merry (1,257), 112

Eat, she says, her rotten bean-curd pancakes, fried in cold water (227), 131

Eighth is (2,207), 65

Even ignorant men seek perfection (1,578), 54

Excitement grips me deep (316), 100

Fair as a flower (Shim 196), 192

Fallen leaves kicked by my horse's hooves (360), 173

Fame I've forgotten (175), 88

Father, to have given me life (955), 127

Feelings of love fuse into fire (1,016), 182

Fifth is (1,484), 64

Fine morning after spring rain (929), 128

Fingers reached to strum the *kŏmun'go* (116), 141

First is (1,729), 63

Fishermen of the Cho River (2,106), 73

Flower, trust not in beauty (154), 176

Flowers bloom when it's hot (646), 94

Flowers bloom within the fence (606), 146

Flowers fall, spring passes (161), 121

Flowers may fall or no (165), 194

Folly, folly (1,437), 129

For a long time now I've known (1,710), 125

Forty thousand boxes of bright jewels (762), 74

Fourth is (993), 64

Friends, let's go flower viewing (1,434), 124

Frost falls on my clothes (1,541), 103

Fuddled with wine as the sun goes
 down (1,133), 37

Gentle sunlight bathes the water (144),
 96
Genuine jade, they said (1,531), 72
Girl, don't be so haughty (42), 176
Girl, I hear you have a field of early rice
 (44), 185
Girl, I've painted a plum tree (50), 189
Girl, look at that flower (Shim 47), 178
Girls, buy all the heat you can (40), 188
Gnarled old stump, black and craggy
 (1,847), 148
Golden crow and jade rabbit (289), 175
Green willows are good (486), 125
Growing old is a grievous pill (539), 177
Grub to cicada (247), 163

Has the dew on the withered leaves
 (69), 154
Has the dew on the withered leaves
 (Shim 80), 172
Have the rigors of winter passed?
 (1,452), 92
Having lived a modest hundred years
 (Shim 1,174), 83
Heart, what is the secret (712), 50
Heaven and earth are parents (2,013),
 126
Herdboy, on the long green grassy
 bank (496), 166
High or low (500), 146
Holding up the hem of her purple
 mantle (1,180), 182
How clean the color of the clouds (222),
 94
How could the heart that loved the
 flower (168), 152
How do you make good wine? (1,253),
 92

How is a house built? (1,943), 91
How many fine silver-jade fish (1,626),
 102
How unspoiled the life of the fisher-
 man (799), 101
How valiant that solitary pine (813), 106
Husband and wife (2,261), 68
Husband dead (402), 75

I asked the lads beneath the pine (1,214),
 82
I awoke from sleep (1,765), 196
I built my thatched hut against a rock
 (1,038), 172
I close my book and open the window
 (1,972), 88
I come to a deserted pavilion (1,603), 62
I cut a branch from the plum (1,521),
 143
I cut a slender willow branch (1,187), 89
I despised the crow for being black out-
 side (Shim 24), 165
I didn't believe you (1,383), 147
I drew a picture of my love (573), 194
I drink till I'm drunk (1,258), 37
I forget as soon as I hear (698), 58
I hang up my fishing line (348), 97
I have been unable to repay the favor of
 the king (244), 127
I lay down at the fishing hole (298), 82
I lay down to sleep that in dreams (251),
 152
I lay my head on the pillow (252), 134
I lie on the bank of the river (78), 60
I live at the foot of the mountain
 (1,042), 166
I long to walk on fragrant grasses (866),
 97
I look up at my snail-shell hut (1,544),
 101

I nodded off; I lost my fishing pole (1,873), 172

I parted from my fair lord (1,987), 45

I plant bamboo; that's my fence (623), 77

I plowed three furrows (380), 86

I promised to return to rivers and lakes (104), 74

I return to Sky-cloud Terrace (1,999), 53

I shake off all the dust of the world (2,327), 143

I sit at the fishing hole (1,948), 76

I sought fame and honor (184), 164

I spy the three-colored peach blossom (1,046), 49

I string my old, neglected *kayagŭm* (840), 93

I thought I was traveling alone (2,323), 169

I urge the children to hurry up (1,337), 132

I wake from a late afternoon nap (1,503), 119

I wanted to forget (553), 192

I want to buy love (1,021), 194

I want to do what is right (1,539), 162

I was born too late to witness (528), 85

I wished to sweep away the clouds that blot the sun (2,222), 139

I wonder a moment (979), 196

Ice crystal, jade bead (992), 147

Iced rice water (1,244), 179

I'd heard of Chirisan's meeting of the waters (686), 55

If a fool, a complete fool (1,382), 161

If, born again in the next life (1,575), 187

If every day could count for (2,246), 151

If everyone were a government official (906), 116

If I laugh to myself (Shim 30), 164

If I lifted my wings (1,481), 71

If strong men fought (84), 118

If the road I walk in my dreams (254), 111

I'll build a house and roof it with clouds (1,944), 169

I'll catch the wild goose (306), 195

I'll cut a piece from the waist (672), 55

I'll cut out my heart (419), 69

I'll draw two characters on a fallen leaf (359), 193

I'll gather all the sharp blades under heaven (2,024), 163

I'll go to my stone hut among the pines (1,218), 104

I'll never forget the boy (64), 134

I'll set a hundred plants (897), 165

I'll spread my nets on the sand (771), 100

I'll take my cares (1,274), 126

I'm a fool at heart (713), 50

I'm an old man now (1,694), 120

I'm building a straw hut beneath a rock (1,045), 91

I'm fifty now, no longer young (77), 67

I'm going now, but meet again we must (2), 197

I'm leaving now (320), 198

I'm like a horse without a bridle (497), 75

I'm up in this lofty tree (479), 62

In a lifespan of a hundred years (1,712), 81

In one hand I grasped a bramble (2,270), 28

In the thick shade of the willow grove (724), 99

In this world medicine is plentiful (1,173), 182

Is anything more hateful (1,734), 165
Is that the cuckoo singing? (1,571), 96
Is the crow black because someone
    dyed it? (22), 166
It is the third watch. The girl in the
    bridal bedroom . . . (667), 190
It's been said from of old (1,969), 106
It's full daylight now (1,485), 69
It's raining; we can't go to the fields
    (986), 92
I've cut a mountain willow, my love
    (774), 112
I've dug and washed (816), 57
I've hung a windbell outside my green
    window (1,955), 172
I've lost youth's rose cheeks (Pak 4,632),
    149
I've plaited a straw hut (2,330), 124
I've taken off my clothes (1,540), 119

Just because you're a beauty (Shim 46),
    178

Last night after the rain (1,424), 85
Last night I slept alone, curled like a
    shrimp (1,423), 180
Lazy I am (429), 91
Leisurely clouds stand on the moun-
    taintop (1,040), 47
Let's drink a cup of wine; let's drink
    another (2,281), 68
Let's play; let's play while we're young
    (478), 176
Letter, do you come alone (2,212), 196
Lie down and I don't want to get up
    (512), 177
Life here is so simple (428), 122
Like a hen-pheasant chased by a hawk
    (330), 193
Like a lotus blossom (26), 134
Listen, my good man (1,675), 69

Listen to me, girl (1,035), 131
Listen to me, lad. Don't be proud
    (1,862), 142
Lone wild goose, crying as you fly
    (2,082), 198
Longing that leads to lovesickness;
    that's a thrill (272), 152
Look at that girl in blouse and pat-
    terned skirt (1,208), 129
Look at the butterfly, how it dances for
    the flower (153), 185
Look down: deep green waters (226),
    47
Lord of creation (1,441), 134
Love is a lie (1,013), 81
Love, why don't you come! (1,410), 191
Lovely the lotus (149), 153
Lying at leisure under my grass roof
    (2,110), 44

Metal I thought, yes (2,032), 155
Mist lifts on the stream in front (1,352),
    95
Moon, round moon, moon that shines
    (597), 181
Moonlight shines on the lotus pond
    (1,922), 128
Moonlight white on white pear blos-
    soms (1,700), 29
Mountain flowers and grasses (2,038),
    113
Mountain valleys, words you have none
    (Shim 169), 166
Mountains may be high (2,196), 49
Mounted on my horse, I visit (1,501), 38
My belly filled with barley and rotten
    shad (923), 124
My dreams were sweet last night (53),
    181
My dreams were sweet last night (58),
    186

My hair may be white (2,204), 129
My heart is restless (Shim 565), 84
My horse is neighing for the road (735), 193
My horse takes fright (737), 173
My house is deep in White Crane Mountain (448), 119
My house is very remote (446), 174
My love has gone; forgotten me, it seems (5), 188
My love is coming! I take dinner early . . . (579), 182
My love said he'd come (578), 187
My sighs will be the breeze (2,275), 187
My soul I'll mingle with wine (440), 140
My straw-roofed hermitage is quite remote (2,121), 120
My thundering love I meet (1,574), 191

Naked children waving spider sticks (857), 144
Neither wood (332), 94
Night comes to a mountain village (1,062), 154
Nights after rain when the moon (1,842), 61
Ninety-nine years old, that old man (1,336), 178
Ninth is (216), 65
North wind bitter through the branches (1,036), 41
Now that I'm keeper of the state guest-house (1,101), 74
Now that I'm keeper of the state guest-house (1,102), 75
Now that I'm keeper of the state guest-house (1,103), 75

Oblivious of net and pole (277), 105

Of all the dogs around me, spotted, black, and hairy (822), 130
Of flying birds and beasts that crawl (980), 183
Of wine in brimming golden jugs (292), 112
Oh youth (1,322), 178
Old and sick (537), 132
Old man fishing (1,142), 173
On my way to Sŏraksan (1,147), 137
On steamy summer dog days (927), 122
On the evidence of last night's encounter (Shim 70), 192
On the road that twists beneath the pines (1,212), 162
On the way to see my love (1,537), 197
One by one I've gathered up my feelings of love (1,020), 181
One sea is hard enough (Pak 4,502), 150
One with the setting sun the ibis flew (2,247), 118
Orioles have willows (Pak 4,687), 149
Out there where the wild geese fly (299), 102

Parting turns to fire (49), 194
Parting turns to fire (1,680), 195
Peace in heaven and on earth (2,202), 58
Peach and plum in the east garden (Shim 888), 151
Peach blossoms fly in the air (655), 146
Peach blossoms in the spring breeze (2,157), 145
Pearly raindrops on green hills (2,066), 67
"People, kind people, please buy my powder and rouge" (644), 165
People of Kangwŏn Province (89), 69

Perhaps I am a magnet (325), 130
Petals fall, new leaves sprout (158), 167
Pick the flower, if you will (Shim 206),
    84
Plum shadows hit the window (743),
    148
Protracted rain comes to an end (233),
    98

Rain clears on rivers and streams (102),
    132
Rain fell in the morning (1,324), 85
Rain plashes the lotus pond (1,921), 76
Red cliffs and green rock faces (583),
    106
Rice wrapped in a green lotus leaf
    (2,104), 47
Ride a horse through a field of flowers
    (738), 179
Ring, you've lost your mate (7), 197
Rip your black robe asunder; fashion a
    pair of breeches (1,793), 191
River village men with nets on your
    shoulders (91), 153
Rowing a skiff alone (2,134), 88

Sad or glad (1,266), 93
Scales judge the light and heavy (264),
    118
Second is (1,633), 64
Set not your sights on fame and honor
    (180), 127
Seventh is (2,173), 64
Shall I put my worries aside (431), 66
Sigh, why do you come to me (2,273),
    197
Sitting on top of Mach'ŏn Pass (715),
    141
Six crock bowls the bride smashed
    (1,100), 184
Sixth is (1,624), 64

Sleep-bound birds fly home (1,776), 71
Snow falling in the pine forest (1,221),
    69
Snow falling on the green mountain
    (2,061), 175
Snow falls on a mountain village (1,061),
    86
So what if I wash my feet (814), 99
Sober I drink again (107), 118
Somehow or other (1,588), 70
Something flickered outside the win-
    dow (1,958), 183
Somewhere on Namsan Mountain
    (383), 70
Sparrows chattering (2,294), 164
Spring breezes blow briefly (2,160),
    175
Spring breezes fill the mountains with
    flowers (2,159), 53
Spring comes to rivers and lakes (100),
    38
Spring comes to rivers and lakes (101),
    39
Spring comes to the countryside (1,829),
    51
Spring comes to the garden (Pak
    4,662), 149
Spring returns (746), 154
Spring visits a farming household
    (1,037), 133
Stock from boiled bitter greens (1,264),
    72
Stop, stop (710), 80
Strains of merry piping delight the ear
    (1,866), 172
Summer clouds, masses of mystery
    peaks (2,250), 142
Summer comes to rivers and lakes (97),
    38
Sun, don't go (2,298), 171

Sunset on the river village (Shim 111), 174

Take all the misfortunes (1,577), 67

Talkers are regarded as idle chatterers (740), 116

Tell me, reverend sir (807), 138

Ten years I've striven (1,309), 50

That boat floating on the autumn river (2,135), 152

That face reflected in the mirror (117), 197

That old man is a free spirit (2,317), 150

The anchor is raised; the boat sails away (609), 198

The ancients cannot see me (145), 54

The blowflies are gone (1,960), 93

The breeze that melted the blue mountain snow (2,060), 28

The clouds have been swept (1,781), 147

The crane sleeping on the pine altar (Shim 1,686), 150

The cuckoo calls; the moon is low on the mountain (2,128), 45

The day is hot (369), 95

The day we parted I cannot say (1,682), 90

The dog barks at the brushwood gate (1,282), 60

The dog barks at the brushwood gate (1,280), 183

The donkey is clearly lame (73), 168

The drum beats in a distant temple (976), 82

The evening sun is grand (1,135), 100

The evening sun slants in the sky (1,136), 96

The first frost of the year turned into wine (781), 176

The fish have left the shallows (1,464), 104

The flower I saw last year (Shim 136), 174

The flowers are about to bloom (152), 128

The flowers have bloomed; the wine is mature (167), 167

The guests have gone; the gate is closed (110), 40

The house behind is made of mud (696), 123

The incense in the golden censer has all burned out (268), 81

The lad has gone to dig fernbrake (1,328), 68

The love that lights my eyes (417), 196

The man who abandons himself to rivers and lakes (99), 143

The mirror I looked at in youth (2,094), 144

The monk grabbed the nun by her hair (1,915), 161

The monk that slept here must, after all, have been a man (1,914), 191

The moon is bright (Shim 1,510), 83

The moon is bright over Hansŏng Pavilion (2,271), 155

The moon is bright tonight, I sit alone (2,267), 77

The moon is clear and round (599), 80

The moon is so bright (601), 169

The moon rises in the Third Watch (1,069), 141

The moon rising above the peak (935), 82

The moon that fades at the end of the month (290), 151

The morning star has set; the lark is on the wing (1,106), 137

The mountain may be high (2,195), 58

The mountains are ancient (1,050), 56

The nine scenic glories of Kosan (142), 63

The northern sky was clear (965), 78

The peach blossoms filling the garden (62), 162

The peony is the king of flowers (766), 123

The pine forest at Kyŏnghoe Pavilion (131), 121

The pursuit of wine and women (1,898), 62

The rain clears over the fishing hole (1,379), 61

The rise and fall of dynasties is in the hands of fate (2,371), 41

The rise and fall of nations are myriad (2,370), 72

The road I once walked (612), 54

The road is long (Shim 79), 172

The searing sun sets on West Mountain (895), 27

The song maker (473), 84

The spring mountain is on fire (2,149), 87

The stream that wept last night (63), 46

The sun goes down; the moon rises (2,301), 147

The sun had all gone down (2,295), 164

The sun sets behind west mountain (1,119), 111

The sun that sets beyond west mountain (362), 134

The talents heaven gave me have been of no avail (1,996), 122

The tree is diseased (331), 66

The trials and tribulations of this life (1,689), 131

The water of ten thousand blue waves (716), 168

The water under Immortals' Bridge (1,146), 33

The white gulls (Shim 2,266), 84

The wild geese have all flown off (304), 137

The wild geese have flown away (305), 195

The wind drives the snow (836), 148

The wind is up; close the lattice door (827), 92

The wind that blew last night (61), 43

The wind that blew open the brushwood gate last night (Shim 73), 192

The world has abandoned me (1,177), 170

The world is bright and buoyant (1,982), 121

There are fragrant orchids in the valley (1,616), 52

There's a terrace in front of the mountain (1,053), 53

They say the moon can see my beloved (600), 194

Third is (1,070), 64

Thirty days in the month (2,258), 58

This old sick body (535), 177

This old sick heart (536), 122

This remote mountain peak (126), 83

Those flowers hidden in East Pavilion (660), 148

Though my body die and die again (1,666), 31

Though thunder topple the mountains (503), 53

Thus I have no worries (1,635), 47

Tiger moth, let me ask you a question (805), 135

Till the wild duck (1,538), 49

Time flows like water (1,182), 139

Tiny object floating high (1,816), 94

Tipsy, I stretch out (2,169), 97

To become a tiger butterfly (2,162), 139

To say simplicity is dead (1,237), 52

To say that growing old is sad (540), 125

To say that the clouds are unwitting (224), 33

To sun and moon (339), 177

Traveler, returning in the night (202), 146

Traveling through the winter scape (88), 189

Trees and grasses wither (2,227), 124

Twilight haze is my home (1,477), 52

Two stone Buddhas, naked and fasting (317), 70

Up on top of Nongam Rock (501), 47

Using a clean-scrubbed pot (1,941), 89

Village people (711), 68

Virtue has lost its burnish (192), 126

Visitors never grace this mountain village (1,060), 128

Warm weather, gentle breezes (1,730), 28

We fixed our tryst for the rising of the moon (1,610), 185

We trained our army—center, right and left (1,073), 125

We'll strain sour wine and drink (1,272), 72

Were I brilliant (1,670), 70

Were it not for coming together in the bridal (Pak 4,666), 149

What about living this way? (1,640), 52

What about living this way? (1,641), 31

What happens if you pull down (1,392), 65

What is fame and honor? (189), 118

What is love like? (1,023), 180

What manner of grub has eaten (1,413), 160

What will I be, you ask (1,665), 43

What's all this about freezing in bed (1,411), 78

What's the point in longing? (281), 186

When autumn leaves are delicate reds (587), 120

When autumn nights are very long (27), 119

When did I ever delight in wine? (435), 170

When did the leaves come out (337), 71

When did the moon come up? (598), 114

When flowers bloom, I think of the moon (166), 133

When I grasp my girl's wrist (45), 182

When I think of you, my love (321), 190

When I was a child I'd clap my hands (1,334), 161

When I was young (340), 176

When I was young and fearless (1,203), 141

When I'm dead and gone (1,664), 186

When my legs give way after drinking wine (1,242), 168

When my love and I parted (575), 198

When our droopy-eared horse (266), 73

When the Great Dipper slips low in the sky (957), 122

When the paulownia leaves fell (751), 74

When the snow cleared last night (59),
    105
When the wine in your house matures
    (1,761), 89
When was I faithless (434), 56
Where do you live? (467), 173
Where is a man sent (1,009), 186
Where is that boat going (2,232), 67
Where the towering mountain slopes
    down to the river (86), 82
Whether I eat wheat bran or rice chaff
    (313), 71
White clouds and blue mist (2,374), 118
White clouds get up (894), 102
White dewdrops angle over the river
    (2,375), 103
White gull (93), 66
White-haired, but wanton still (880),
    185
White heron beside the stream (457),
    85
White heron, do not go (18), 32
White heron, do not mock (15), 30
White heron, standing on that empty
    boat (978), 144
White snow fills all heaven and earth
    (888), 174
Who can build a fine big house (505),
    136
Who can tell how wind and waves will
    change (860), 100
Who pierced the paper window?
    (1,946), 170
Who says I am old? (525), 151
Who says the bamboo bent in the
    snow (515), 41
Who says the crow (524), 139
Who sliced the crescent moon so small
    (2,117), 113
Why are green mountains (2,065), 54

Why are blue mountains (2,064), 116
Why do flowers fall (157), 94
Why do grasses and trees (930), 133
Why do insects cry in the grass (76),
    185
Why does that pine tree stand (1,858),
    66
Why is spring so late (2,042), 40
Why is the sky round (2,242), 126
Wild beasts know cold and warmth
    (Shim 380), 138
Wild geese light on the broad sweep of
    sand (2,213), 59
Wild goose, alarmed by autumn frost
    (2,140), 59
Wild goose crying as you fly (1,117), 140
Wild goose, soaring in the blue (2,086),
    195
Will sleep come if I lie down (513), 186
Will there be no tomorrow (439), 98
Wind blowing gently athwart (469),
    102
Wind rises in the pondweed (709), 98
Winds rest before crossing that ridge
    (825), 190
Wine cup in hand I open the window
    (589), 167
Wine cup in hand, I sit alone (1,772), 91
Wine drowsiness wears thin (1,238), 145
Wine without virtue (1,239), 92
Wine, why do you redden (1,251), 170
Winter comes to rivers and lakes (96),
    39
Winter sunlight falls thick (221),
    104
With my sharp knife I cut a length of
    light (29), 198
With no calendar in the hills (1,057),
    171
With nothing to do (1,671), 143

With tears I beg you; don't brush aside (1,593), 188

With the blood from my wounded heart (410), 85

With the new moon hanging (1,092), 83

With yellow chrysanthemums newly bloomed (1,091), 50

Within the higher ranks of the military office (1,831), 130

Woman, your face once beautiful is like that red willow tree (48), 189

Wordless the blue mountains (733), 63

Would that my love were a paulownia tree (569), 136

Wrap my rice in lotus leaves (1,469), 98

Yesterday I heard that Master Sŏng (1,811), 70

Yesterday a flower bloomed (1,771), 136

You ask how many friends I have? (423), 93

You ask what I (2,220), 142

You beg a man like me who wouldn't eat honey cakes (310), 189

You have indeed bloomed (520), 147

You may extol fame and honor (178), 126

You may like blue clouds (2,076), 127

You men with guns on the riverbank (80), 195

You who are drunk on bureaucratic ambition (2,344), 123

Young men in your prime (2,092), 175

Your teeth gleam when you smile (1,597), 192

You're no sooner here than you want to go (1,500), 79

# Harvard East Asian Monographs
(* out-of-print)

*1.  Liang Fang-chung, *The Single-Whip Method of Taxation in China*

*2.  Harold C. Hinton, *The Grain Tribute System of China, 1845–1911*

3.  Ellsworth C. Carlson, *The Kaiping Mines, 1877–1912*

*4.  Chao Kuo-chün, *Agrarian Policies of Mainland China: A Documentary Study, 1949–1956*

*5.  Edgar Snow, *Random Notes on Red China, 1936–1945*

*6.  Edwin George Beal, Jr., *The Origin of Likin, 1835–1864*

7.  Chao Kuo-chün, *Economic Planning and Organization in Mainland China: A Documentary Study, 1949–1957*

*8.  John K. Fairbank, *Ching Documents: An Introductory Syllabus*

*9.  Helen Yin and Yi-chang Yin, *Economic Statistics of Mainland China, 1949–1957*

*10.  Wolfgang Franke, *The Reform and Abolition of the Traditional Chinese Examination System*

11.  Albert Feuerwerker and S. Cheng, *Chinese Communist Studies of Modern Chinese History*

12.  C. John Stanley, *Late Ching Finance: Hu Kuang-yung as an Innovator*

13.  S. M. Meng, *The Tsungli Yamen: Its Organization and Functions*

*14.  Ssu-yü Teng, *Historiography of the Taiping Rebellion*

15.  Chun-Jo Liu, *Controversies in Modern Chinese Intellectual History: An Analytic Bibliography of Periodical Articles, Mainly of the May Fourth and Post–May Fourth Era*

*16.  Edward J. M. Rhoads, *The Chinese Red Army, 1927–1963: An Annotated Bibliography*

17.  Andrew J. Nathan, *A History of the China International Famine Relief Commission*

*18.  Frank H. H. King (ed.) and Prescott Clarke, *A Research Guide to China-Coast Newspapers, 1822–1911*

19.  Ellis Joffe, *Party and Army: Professionalism and Political Control in the Chinese Officer Corps, 1949–1964*

*20.  Toshio G. Tsukahira, *Feudal Control in Tokugawa Japan: The Sankin Kōtai System*

21.  Kwang-Ching Liu, ed., *American Missionaries in China: Papers from Harvard Seminars*

22.  George Moseley, *A Sino-Soviet Cultural Frontier: The Ili Kazakh Autonomous Chou*

# Harvard East Asian Monographs

23. Carl F. Nathan, *Plague Prevention and Politics in Manchuria, 1910–1931*

*24. Adrian Arthur Bennett, *John Fryer: The Introduction of Western Science and Technology into Nineteenth-Century China*

25. Donald J. Friedman, *The Road from Isolation: The Campaign of the American Committee for Non-Participation in Japanese Aggression, 1938–1941*

*26. Edward LeFevour, *Western Enterprise in Late Ching China: A Selective Survey of Jardine, Matheson and Company's Operations, 1842–1895*

27. Charles Neuhauser, *Third World Politics: China and the Afro-Asian People's Solidarity Organization, 1957–1967*

28. Kungtu C. Sun, assisted by Ralph W. Huenemann, *The Economic Development of Manchuria in the First Half of the Twentieth Century*

*29. Shahid Javed Burki, *A Study of Chinese Communes, 1965*

30. John Carter Vincent, *The Extraterritorial System in China: Final Phase*

31. Madeleine Chi, *China Diplomacy, 1914–1918*

*32. Clifton Jackson Phillips, *Protestant America and the Pagan World: The First Half Century of the American Board of Commissioners for Foreign Missions, 1810–1860*

33. James Pusey, *Wu Han: Attacking the Present through the Past*

34. Ying-wan Cheng, *Postal Communication in China and Its Modernization, 1860–1896*

35. Tuvia Blumenthal, *Saving in Postwar Japan*

36. Peter Frost, *The Bakumatsu Currency Crisis*

37. Stephen C. Lockwood, *Augustine Heard and Company, 1858–1862*

38. Robert R. Campbell, *James Duncan Campbell: A Memoir by His Son*

39. Jerome Alan Cohen, ed., *The Dynamics of China's Foreign Relations*

40. V. V. Vishnyakova-Akimova, *Two Years in Revolutionary China, 1925–1927,* tr. Steven L. Levine

*41. Meron Medzini, *French Policy in Japan during the Closing Years of the Tokugawa Regime*

42. Ezra Vogel, Margie Sargent, Vivienne B. Shue, Thomas Jay Mathews, and Deborah S. Davis, *The Cultural Revolution in the Provinces*

*43. Sidney A. Forsythe, *An American Missionary Community in China, 1895–1905*

*44. Benjamin I. Schwartz, ed., *Reflections on the May Fourth Movement.: A Symposium*

*45. Ching Young Choe, *The Rule of the Taewŏngun, 1864–1873: Restoration in Yi Korea*

46. W. P. J. Hall, *A Bibliographical Guide to Japanese Research on the Chinese Economy, 1958–1970*

47. Jack J. Gerson, *Horatio Nelson Lay and Sino-British Relations, 1854–1864*

48. Paul Richard Bohr, *Famine and the Missionary: Timothy Richard as Relief Administrator and Advocate of National Reform*

49. Endymion Wilkinson, *The History of Imperial China: A Research Guide*

50. Britten Dean, *China and Great Britain: The Diplomacy of Commercial Relations, 1860–1864*

51. Ellsworth C. Carlson, *The Foochow Missionaries, 1847–1880*

# Harvard East Asian Monographs

52. Yeh-chien Wang, *An Estimate of the Land-Tax Collection in China, 1753 and 1908*

53. Richard M. Pfeffer, *Understanding Business Contracts in China, 1949–1963*

54. Han-sheng Chuan and Richard Kraus, *Mid-Ching Rice Markets and Trade: An Essay in Price History*

55. Ranbir Vohra, *Lao She and the Chinese Revolution*

56. Liang-lin Hsiao, *China's Foreign Trade Statistics, 1864–1949*

*57. Lee-hsia Hsu Ting, *Government Control of the Press in Modern China, 1900–1949*

58. Edward W. Wagner, *The Literati Purges: Political Conflict in Early Yi Korea*

*59. Joungwon A. Kim, *Divided Korea: The Politics of Development, 1945–1972*

*60. Noriko Kamachi, John K. Fairbank, and Chūzō Ichiko, *Japanese Studies of Modern China Since 1953: A Bibliographical Guide to Historical and Social-Science Research on the Nineteenth and Twentieth Centuries, Supplementary Volume for 1953–1969*

61. Donald A. Gibbs and Yun-chen Li, *A Bibliography of Studies and Translations of Modern Chinese Literature, 1918–1942*

62. Robert H. Silin, *Leadership and Values: The Organization of Large-Scale Taiwanese Enterprises*

63. David Pong, *A Critical Guide to the Kwangtung Provincial Archives Deposited at the Public Record Office of London*

*64. Fred W. Drake, *China Charts the World: Hsu Chi-yü and His Geography of 1848*

*65. William A. Brown and Urgrunge Onon, translators and annotators, *History of the Mongolian People's Republic*

66. Edward L. Farmer, *Early Ming Government: The Evolution of Dual Capitals*

*67. Ralph C. Croizier, *Koxinga and Chinese Nationalism: History, Myth, and the Hero*

*68. William J. Tyler, tr., *The Psychological World of Natsume Sōseki*, by Doi Takeo

69. Eric Widmer, *The Russian Ecclesiastical Mission in Peking during the Eighteenth Century*

*70. Charlton M. Lewis, *Prologue to the Chinese Revolution: The Transformation of Ideas and Institutions in Hunan Province, 1891–1907*

71. Preston Torbert, *The Ching Imperial Household Department: A Study of Its Organization and Principal Functions, 1662–1796*

72. Paul A. Cohen and John E. Schrecker, eds., *Reform in Nineteenth-Century China*

73. Jon Sigurdson, *Rural Industrialism in China*

74. Kang Chao, *The Development of Cotton Textile Production in China*

75. Valentin Rabe, *The Home Base of American China Missions, 1880–1920*

*76. Sarasin Viraphol, *Tribute and Profit: Sino-Siamese Trade, 1652–1853*

77. Ch'i-ch'ing Hsiao, *The Military Establishment of the Yuan Dynasty*

78. Meishi Tsai, *Contemporary Chinese Novels and Short Stories, 1949–1974: An Annotated Bibliography*

*79. Wellington K. K. Chan, *Merchants, Mandarins and Modern Enterprise in Late Ching China*

# Harvard East Asian Monographs

80. Endymion Wilkinson, *Landlord and Labor in Late Imperial China: Case Studies from Shandong by Jing Su and Luo Lun*

*81. Barry Keenan, *The Dewey Experiment in China: Educational Reform and Political Power in the Early Republic*

*82. George A. Hayden, *Crime and Punishment in Medieval Chinese Drama: Three Judge Pao Plays*

*83. Sang-Chul Suh, *Growth and Structural Changes in the Korean Economy, 1910–1940*

84. J. W. Dower, *Empire and Aftermath: Yoshida Shigeru and the Japanese Experience, 1878–1954*

85. Martin Collcutt, *Five Mountains: The Rinzai Zen Monastic Institution in Medieval Japan*

86. Kwang Suk Kim and Michael Roemer, *Growth and Structural Transformation*

87. Anne O. Krueger, *The Developmental Role of the Foreign Sector and Aid*

*88. Edwin S. Mills and Byung-Nak Song, *Urbanization and Urban Problems*

89. Sung Hwan Ban, Pal Yong Moon, and Dwight H. Perkins, *Rural Development*

*90. Noel F. McGinn, Donald R. Snodgrass, Yung Bong Kim, Shin-Bok Kim, and Quee-Young Kim, *Education and Development in Korea*

91. Leroy P. Jones and Il SaKong, *Government, Business, and Entrepreneurship in Economic Development: The Korean Case*

92. Edward S. Mason, Dwight H. Perkins, Kwang Suk Kim, David C. Cole, Mahn Je Kim et al., *The Economic and Social Modernization of the Republic of Korea*

93. Robert Repetto, Tai Hwan Kwon, Son-Ung Kim, Dae Young Kim, John E. Sloboda, and Peter J. Donaldson, *Economic Development, Population Policy, and Demographic Transition in the Republic of Korea*

94. Parks M. Coble, Jr., *The Shanghai Capitalists and the Nationalist Government, 1927–1937*

95. Noriko Kamachi, *Reform in China: Huang Tsun-hsien and the Japanese Model*

96. Richard Wich, *Sino-Soviet Crisis Politics: A Study of Political Change and Communication*

97. Lillian M. Li, *China's Silk Trade: Traditional Industry in the Modern World, 1842–1937*

98. R. David Arkush, *Fei Xiaotong and Sociology in Revolutionary China*

*99. Kenneth Alan Grossberg, *Japan's Renaissance: The Politics of the Muromachi Bakufu*

100. James Reeve Pusey, *China and Charles Darwin*

101. Hoyt Cleveland Tillman, *Utilitarian Confucianism: Chen Liang's Challenge to Chu Hsi*

102. Thomas A. Stanley, *Ōsugi Sakae, Anarchist in Taishō Japan: The Creativity of the Ego*

103. Jonathan K. Ocko, *Bureaucratic Reform in Provincial China: Ting Jih-ch'ang in Restoration Kiangsu, 1867–1870*

104. James Reed, *The Missionary Mind and American East Asia Policy, 1911–1915*

105. Neil L. Waters, *Japan's Local Pragmatists: The Transition from Bakumatsu to Meiji in the Kawasaki Region*

106. David C. Cole and Yung Chul Park, *Financial Development in Korea, 1945–1978*

# Harvard East Asian Monographs

107. Roy Bahl, Chuk Kyo Kim, and Chong Kee Park, *Public Finances during the Korean Modernization Process*

108. William D. Wray, *Mitsubishi and the N.Y.K, 1870–1914: Business Strategy in the Japanese Shipping Industry*

109. Ralph William Huenemann, *The Dragon and the Iron Horse: The Economics of Railroads in China, 1876–1937*

110. Benjamin A. Elman, *From Philosophy to Philology: Intellectual and Social Aspects of Change in Late Imperial China*

111. Jane Kate Leonard, *Wei Yüan and China's Rediscovery of the Maritime World*

112. Luke S. K. Kwong, *A Mosaic of the Hundred Days:. Personalities, Politics, and Ideas of 1898*

113. John E. Wills, Jr., *Embassies and Illusions: Dutch and Portuguese Envoys to K'ang-hsi, 1666–1687*

114. Joshua A. Fogel, *Politics and Sinology: The Case of Naitō Konan (1866–1934)*

*115. Jeffrey C. Kinkley, ed., *After Mao: Chinese Literature and Society, 1978– 1981*

116. C. Andrew Gerstle, *Circles of Fantasy: Convention in the Plays of Chikamatsu*

117. Andrew Gordon, *The Evolution of Labor Relations in Japan: Heavy Industry, 1853–1955*

*118. Daniel K. Gardner, *Chu Hsi and the "Ta Hsueh": Neo-Confucian Reflection on the Confucian Canon*

119. Christine Guth Kanda, *Shinzō: Hachiman Imagery and Its Development*

*120. Robert Borgen, *Sugawara no Michizane and the Early Heian Court*

121. Chang-tai Hung, *Going to the People: Chinese Intellectual and Folk Literature, 1918–1937*

* 122. Michael A. Cusumano, *The Japanese Automobile Industry: Technology and Management at Nissan and Toyota*

123. Richard von Glahn, *The Country of Streams and Grottoes: Expansion, Settlement, and the Civilizing of the Sichuan Frontier in Song Times*

124. Steven D. Carter, *The Road to Komatsubara: A Classical Reading of the Renga Hyakuin*

125. Katherine F. Bruner, John K. Fairbank, and Richard T. Smith, *Entering China's Service: Robert Hart's Journals, 1854–1863*

126. Bob Tadashi Wakabayashi, *Anti-Foreignism and Western Learning in Early-Modern Japan: The "New Theses" of 1825*

127. Atsuko Hirai, *Individualism and Socialism: The Life and Thought of Kawai Eijirō (1891–1944)*

128. Ellen Widmer, *The Margins of Utopia: "Shui-hu hou-chuan" and the Literature of Ming Loyalism*

129. R. Kent Guy, *The Emperor's Four Treasuries: Scholars and the State in the Late Chien-lung Era*

130. Peter C. Perdue, *Exhausting the Earth: State and Peasant in Hunan, 1500–1850*

131. Susan Chan Egan, *A Latterday Confucian: Reminiscences of William Hung (1893–1980)*

132. James T. C. Liu, *China Turning Inward: Intellectual-Political Changes in the Early Twelfth Century*

# Harvard East Asian Monographs

133. Paul A. Cohen, *Between Tradition and Modernity: Wang T'ao and Reform in Late Ching China*

134. Kate Wildman Nakai, *Shogunal Politics: Arai Hakuseki and the Premises of Tokugawa Rule*

135. Parks M. Coble, *Facing Japan: Chinese Politics and Japanese Imperialism, 1931–1937*

136. Jon L. Saari, *Legacies of Childhood: Growing Up Chinese in a Time of Crisis, 1890–1920*

137. Susan Downing Videen, *Tales of Heichū*

138. Heinz Morioka and Miyoko Sasaki, *Rakugo: The Popular Narrative Art of Japan*

139. Joshua A. Fogel, *Nakae Ushikichi in China: The Mourning of Spirit*

140. Alexander Barton Woodside, *Vietnam and the Chinese Model.: A Comparative Study of Vietnamese and Chinese Government in the First Half of the Nineteenth Century*

141. George Elision, *Deus Destroyed: The Image of Christianity in Early Modern Japan*

142. William D. Wray, ed., *Managing Industrial Enterprise: Cases from Japan's Prewar Experience*

143. T'ung-tsu Ch'ü, *Local Government in China under the Ching*

144. Marie Anchordoguy, *Computers, Inc.: Japan's Challenge to IBM*

145. Barbara Molony, *Technology and Investment: The Prewar Japanese Chemical Industry*

146. Mary Elizabeth Berry, *Hideyoshi*

147. Laura E. Hein, *Fueling Growth: The Energy Revolution and Economic Policy in Postwar Japan*

148. Wen-hsin Yeh, *The Alienated Academy: Culture and Politics in Republican China, 1919–1937*

149. Dru C. Gladney, *Muslim Chinese: Ethnic Nationalism in the People's Republic*

150. Merle Goldman and Paul A. Cohen, eds., *Ideas Across Cultures: Essays on Chinese Thought in Honor of Benjamin L Schwartz*

151. James Polachek, *The Inner Opium War*

152. Gail Lee Bernstein, *Japanese Marxist: A Portrait of Kawakami Hajime, 1879–1946*

153. Lloyd E. Eastman, *The Abortive Revolution: China under Nationalist Rule, 1927–1937*

154. Mark Mason, *American Multinationals and Japan: The Political Economy of Japanese Capital Controls, 1899–1980*

155. Richard J. Smith, John K. Fairbank, and Katherine F. Bruner, *Robert Hart and China's Early Modernization: His Journals, 1863–1866*

156. George J. Tanabe, Jr., *Myōe the Dreamkeeper: Fantasy and Knowledge in Kamakura Buddhism*

157. William Wayne Farris, *Heavenly Warriors: The Evolution of Japan's Military, 500–1300*

158. Yu-ming Shaw, *An American Missionary in China: John Leighton Stuart and Chinese-American Relations*

159. James B. Palais, *Politics and Policy in Traditional Korea*

160. Douglas Reynolds, *China, 1898–1912: The Xinzheng Revolution and Japan*

161. Roger Thompson, *China's Local Councils in the Age of Constitutional Reform*

162. William Johnston, *The Modern Epidemic: History of Tuberculosis in Japan*

# Harvard East Asian Monographs

163.  Constantine Nomikos Vaporis, *Breaking Barriers: Travel and the State in Early Modern Japan*

164.  Irmela Hijiya-Kirschnereit, *Rituals of Self-Revelation: Shishōsetsu as Literary Genre and Socio-Cultural Phenomenon*

165.  James C. Baxter, *The Meiji Unification through the Lens of Ishikawa Prefecture*

166.  Thomas R. H. Havens, *Architects of Affluence: The Tsutsumi Family and the Seibu-Saison Enterprises in Twentieth-Century Japan*

167.  Anthony Hood Chambers, *The Secret Window: Ideal Worlds in Tanizaki's Fiction*

168.  Steven J. Ericson, *The Sound of the Whistle: Railroads and the State in Meiji Japan*

169.  Andrew Edmund Goble, *Kenmu: Go-Daigo's Revolution*

170.  Denise Potrzeba Lett, *In Pursuit of Status: The Making of South Korea's "New" Urban Middle Class*

171.  Mimi Hall Yiengpruksawan, *Hiraizumi: Buddhist Art and Regional Politics in Twelfth-Century Japan*

172.  Charles Shirō Inouye, *The Similitude of Blossoms: A Critical Biography of Izumi Kyōka (1873–1939), Japanese Novelist and Playwright*

173.  Aviad E. Raz, *Riding the Black Ship: Japan and Tokyo Disneyland*

174.  Deborah J. Milly, *Poverty, Equality, and Growth: The Politics of Economic Need in Postwar Japan*

175.  See Heng Teow, *Japan's Cultural Policy Toward China, 1918–1931: A Comparative Perspective*

176.  Michael A. Fuller, *An Introduction to Literary Chinese*

177.  Frederick R. Dickinson, *War and National Reinvention: Japan in the Great War, 1914–1919*

178.  John Solt, *Shredding the Tapestry of Meaning: The Poetry and Poetics of Kitasono Katue (1902–1978)*

179.  Edward Pratt, *Japan's Protoindustrial Elite: The Economic Foundations of the Gōnō*

180.  Atsuko Sakaki, *Recontextualizing Texts: Narrative Performance in Modern Japanese Fiction*

181.  Soon-Won Park, *Colonial Industrialization and Labor in Korea: The Onoda Cement Factory*

182.  JaHyun Kim Haboush and Martina Deuchler, *Culture and the State in Late Chosŏn Korea*

183.  John W. Chaffee, *Branches of Heaven: A History of the Imperial Clan of Sung China*

184.  Gi-Wook Shin and Michael Robinson, eds., *Colonial Modernity in Korea*

185.  Nam-lin Hur, *Prayer and Play in Late Tokugawa Japan: Asakusa Sensōji and Edo Society*

186.  Kristin Stapleton, *Civilizing Chengdu: Chinese Urban Reform, 1895–1937*

187.  Hyung Il Pai, *Constructing "Korean" Origins: A Critical Review of Archaeology, Historiography, and Racial Myth in Korean State-Formation Theories*

188.  Brian D. Ruppert, *Jewel in the Ashes: Buddha Relics and Power in Early Medieval Japan*

189.  Susan Daruvala, *Zhou Zuoren and an Alternative Chinese Response to Modernity*

# Harvard East Asian Monographs

190. James Z. Lee, *The Political Economy of a Frontier: Southwest China, 1250–1850*

191. Kerry Smith, *A Time of Crisis: Japan, the Great Depression, and Rural Revitalization*

192. Michael Lewis, *Becoming Apart: National Power and Local Politics in Toyama, 1868–1945*

193. William C. Kirby, Man-houng Lin, James Chin Shih, and David A. Pietz, eds., *State and Economy in Republican China: A Handbook for Scholars*

194. Timothy S. George, *Minamata: Pollution and the Struggle for Democracy in Postwar Japan*

195. Billy K. L. So, *Prosperity, Region, and Institutions in Maritime China: The South Fukien Pattern, 946–1368*

196. Yoshihisa Tak Matsusaka, *The Making of Japanese Manchuria, 1904–1932*

197. Maram Epstein, *Competing Discourses: Orthodoxy, Authenticity, and Engendered Meanings in Late Imperial Chinese Fiction*

198. Curtis J. Milhaupt, J. Mark Ramseyer, and Michael K. Young, eds. and comps., *Japanese Law in Context: Readings in Society, the Economy, and Politics*

199. Haruo Iguchi, *Unfinished Business: Ayukawa Yoshisuke and U.S.-Japan Relations, 1937–1952*

200. Scott Pearce, Audrey Spiro, and Patricia Ebrey, *Culture and Power in the Reconstitution of the Chinese Realm, 200–600*

201. Terry Kawashima, *Writing Margins: The Textual Construction of Gender in Heian and Kamakura Japan*

202. Martin W. Huang, *Desire and Fictional Narrative in Late Imperial China*

203. Robert S. Ross and Jiang Changbin, eds., *Re-examining the Cold War: U.S.-China Diplomacy, 1954–1973*

204. Guanhua Wang, *In Search of Justice: The 1905–1906 Chinese Anti-American Boycott*

205. David Schaberg, *A Patterned Past: Form and Thought in Early Chinese Historiography*

206. Christine Yano, *Tears of Longing: Nostalgia and the Nation in Japanese Popular Song*

207. Milena Doleželová-Velingerová and Oldřich Král, with Graham Sanders, eds., *The Appropriation of Cultural Capital: China's May Fourth Project*

208. Robert N. Huey, *The Making of 'Shinkokinshū'*

209. Lee Butler, *Emperor and Aristocracy in Japan, 1467–1680: Resilience and Renewal*

210. Suzanne Odgen, *Inklings of Democracy in China*

211. Kenneth J. Ruoff, *The People's Emperor: Democracy and the Japanese Monarchy, 1945–1995*

212. Haun Saussy, *Great Walls of Discourse and Other Adventures in Cultural China*

213. Aviad E. Raz, *Emotions at Work: Normative Control, Organizations, and Culture in Japan and America*

214. Rebecca E. Karl and Peter Zarrow, eds., *Rethinking the 1898 Reform Period: Political and Cultural Change in Late Qing China*

215. Kevin O'Rourke, *The Book of Korean Shijo*